PLOTTING YOUR STORY ARC

Workbook For Fiction Writers, Plotters and Pantsers

Nancy Brophy

Plotting Your Story Arc,
Workbook for Fiction Writers, Plotters and Pantsers
Copyright©2014
Nancy Brophy

ISBN 978-0-9862354-0-5

Cover Design by Susan Lute
www.susanlute.com

Thanks to the following people: Susan Lute, Lynn Jordan, Linda Kaye and Jessica Smith for all their help and guidance. Not only have these women been fabulous friends, each is a writer worthy of note. To these ladies I raise my glass with the Irish toast:

> There are good ships,
>
> And there are wood ships.
>
> The ships that sail the sea.
>
> But the best ships, are friendships,
>
> And may they always be.

Let no one distract you from your goals.

Continue to write even if your internal editor tells you to quit.

Persist. The middle of anything looks like failure.

Production is more important than perfection.

Passion is mandatory.

The paperwork is endless.

The rewards are worth it.

TABLE OF CONTENTS

Heroine

The Villain, the Nemesis, The Antagonist

Example

About the Author

INTRODUCTION

"The role of a writer is not to say what we all can say, but what we are unable to say."
-Anaïs Nin

USING THIS WORKBOOK

There are published writers who plot, write detailed synopses, outline, or have waking dreams about their story. There are also those who do not. They sit at their computers and start at page one and write until the book is done. Others puzzle a book together like a jigsaw, writing a segment here and a segment there.

JK Rowling developed her stories with ideas for each grade level jotted on scraps of paper and dropped into the various boxes each representing a different school year.

Every author has a unique procedure and many have a different process for every book. There are those who claim they cannot write the story if they know what's going to happen and those who can't write the story unless they do. As a novelist you fall somewhere on this continuum.

This workbook can be used by either. However, since I am a pantser (one who writes by the seat of their pants) I designed this workbook based upon the way I write.

The secrets to the Universe are not contained within these pages. Nor have I gone into depth on any one topic in particular. This workbook is designed to jog your memory into editing mode when your heart would prefer to sink into the actions and lives of your characters.

There are checklists, exercises, outlines and even scrapbooking. One can utilize these work pages before writing a single word as a plotting exercise or (like me) wait until the middle when the writer has lost sight of where he/she means to go. Others might finish the manuscript and then rely on this material for final editing.

As a romance writer I recognize that genre writing has different requirements than other fiction writing and I have tried to note those where I thought it was particularly helpful.

Many authors need visual aids when they are constructing the characters and location. Included are blank pages for your cover, photos of characters, maps or drawings of story locations, notes about research and a working grid to keep track of the number of words written each day and how many days of the month you plan to write.

Thank you for purchasing this workbook. If you have additions, edits or ideas, contact me. Also note that each page is copyrighted.

Nancy Brophy
Nancybrophy@gmail.com

"The only place success comes before work is the dictionary."
-Vincent "Vince" Lombardi

SECRETS TO WRITING

What's the most important advice any author can give another?

Write the damn book.

You can purchase a thousand how-to books including this one and it will not help you if you do not put your butt in a chair and crank out a first draft. You must finish a manuscript even if you don't know a single rule of grammar. Whether you've written an extensive synopsis or plotted every scene or been driven crazy by voices in your head, if you do not put the words on the page, nothing else will matter. This book like so many others will not help you. Unless you are a person who likes rooms decorated with books on shelves, then it will look lovely resting next to others. And your decorating dreams will be fulfilled.

Do not worry about publishing. Do not worry about style. Write the damn book. It can be revised and edited when you've finished. Nora Roberts is famously quoted as having said, "I can edit anything but a blank page." The difference between a good book and a great book is only a few sentences. This workbook will help you've include everything you need.

Everyone thinks they have a novel in them. No, make that a best-seller. But they don't. Because they underestimate the skill good writing takes. Not only is it difficult to find the time to get the words on the page, it is even harder to get them in the right order.

Most writers spend years learning the craft. We've studied books, taken classes, entered contests, and forced our friends and family into reading rough drafts. Critique groups have shaped one or more novels. We've storyboarded, plotted, cut and pasted, edited and re-edited.

There are a lot of ways to look busy and not write.

Sometimes you have to slay your inner demons by giving them to one of your characters. Well-meaning friends and family all have opinions, but your words are your words. You have to have the confidence to bend in the wind without whirling like a weather vane.

Every writing book has taught me something about story arc, character development, conflict, character emotion, layering, editing and time management. But the basic thing I've learned is that all the knowledge in the world doesn't get words on the page. The only solution for that, regardless of where you are on the continuum of your writing career, is to put your butt in a chair, hunch over your computer and…

Write. Write. Write.

"It took me fifteen years to discover I had no talent for writing, but I couldn't give it up because by that time I was too famous." - Robert Benchley

RULES FOR FICTION WRITING

There are no rules. So why write a book that - for better or worse - is mainly ruled based? There was a time when New York Publishers set the rules and we writers followed them if we had even a hope of being published.

Once an author was established and had a fan-base they were less restricted. Nora Roberts is renowned for head hopping (more than one POV per scene). George RR Martin does everything wrong. He kills off characters for no other reason than he can. He has a dozen or more POV characters and has annoyed countless fans because he does not write faster. Tolkien edited and re-edited The Hobbit long after it was originally published to make The Lord of the Rings work as a sequel.

Despite the adage there are no rules, there are definite paths others have taken before you. You might be a machete-owning fool who insists upon blazing a new trail, but if your 'original approach' throws the reader out of the story, they might never finish the book and find out how truly brilliant you are.

Character counts. Emotion counts. Story counts.

No one can tell an author what to do or how to make their story work. One of the best rules was written by Kurt Vonnegut. *Use the time of a total stranger in such a way that he or she will not feel the time was wasted.*

Others will caution you to not let your mother read over your shoulder, meaning don't censor your book because your mother or others might not approve.

Writing is a profession where the author has chance after chance to improve. With each book there is a lesson (or more) to be learned. While it is a solitary endeavor, others can help light the path.

Find a critique partner(s). Join a writing group.
Take classes.
Read. Read. Read.
Set a schedule.
Protect your writing time.
Don't let your family interfere.
Turn off the internet.
Forget about the closet that needs to be reorganized.
Believe in yourself.
Finish what you start.
When complete do not shove it under the bed or save it to a secure backup system.
Market it.
Develop a thick skin.
Get it published.
Begin again.

"I'm standing on the edge of the cliff waiting for someone to build a bridge and refusing to acknowledge that I can fly." -Wendy Warren

SELF-DEFEATING BEHAVIOR

Someone ought to do a reality show called A Thousand Ways to Defeat Yourself. We all do it. And we all have our special little twist on how we take aim and fire at our own feet. You may think that I see myself as a sage, able to dispense advice freely because my life is so perfect. However, I didn't write this for you, in truth I wrote this to remind myself to stay on the path and not wander into the woods.

1) **Finish the manuscript**. A story is easy to start. I am the self-appointed queen of 70-100 pages. I have the concept of a cute meet down. But a story is more than a cute meet and these characters must become my best friends. I have to like them. I have to be able to root for them even as I'm throwing them under the bus.

2) **Edit.** I am so excited when a story comes together and I can finally write the words 'The End'. If I've already won the gold, why am I re-running the race? The phrase 'good writing is in the rewriting' came about because editing is as difficult as writing the original draft. Cut, rewrite, reshape. Get feedback. Cut, rewrite, reshape.

3) **Volunteer time**. The writing community is fun. My friends are other writers. People talk about their books, their successes and failures. It's easy to rub shoulders with famous and almost famous people. I'm able to live vicariously through others. Plus everyone is so grateful that I'm doing the volunteer things they want to do, but don't have the time – because they are producing – they are writing.

4) **Write. Write. Write** – Write the blog. Write the website. Write on the Facebook wall. Tweet. We spend hours writing everything but the manuscript.

5) **Never consider alternatives.** E-pubbed? Self-pubbed? A different genre? A different length?

6) **Never let others see your work until it is perfect** because they might make a comment that re-enforces old insecurities and the secret belief that every story could have been better told by an illiterate five-year-old.

7) **Stop doing the things I need to do,** such as writing, sending work out, entering contests, going to conferences, interacting with other writers, learning and relearning craft.

8) **Refuse to pay someone to do what I can't or won't** – copyediting, covers, formatting.

9) **Refuse to take action** – if my book isn't selling, maybe it's the title or cover or marketing needs help.

10) **Refuse to face my fears**. The voice in your head that says I'm not good enough, wins. What was I thinking for even trying?

11) **Dream instead of working**. I once read writers are liars. They make stories up and manipulate the events to have the outcome they desire. Some of us believe we can do that with our own lives. We tell ourselves that we are slow writers and that nineteen games of mindless spider solitaire is really how we plot. We wait for the muses. We refused to treat writing like a regular career and requires real time and serious work.

"Either write something worth reading or do something worth writing." -Benjamin Franklin

WHY DO WE WRITE?

Why do we write? For each of us there is a different answer to that question. And frankly, we don't need a one size fits all placebo. But we do need to understand our own whys.

W – What do you want?

This is an amazingly hard question to answer.

What do you want? To be famous? To publish with New York? To be rich? To make the NYT best seller list? To get the story out of your head and onto paper? To become the best writer you can be? Are you serious about writing? Or is this just a fun exercise? Are you treating it like a real job, even if you are only doing it part-time?

H – How are you going to get it?

Well, first and foremost, you've got to finish the damn book.

If you don't know what you want, how are you going to know when you get it? Are you giving up if you don't meet your goals with the first book? In order to succeed you must have a strong why. Because, while these are simple steps, it is not simple work. Completing the manuscript is not easy. And neither is the editing and rewriting that follow. What else are you prepared to do? Self-publish? Design a cover? Market?

Y – What is your responsibility for getting it?

Lots of us have goals – real and imaginary. (No matter how much you want it to be – winning the lottery is not a real goal). Many of us have gone beyond dreaming. We've stated what we want and posted it on the bathroom mirror. But how many of us have self-restrictive rules that usually begin with "I can't do that because…"

We have lives. Children, spouses, jobs. These are things to which you're also committed. Second to completing the damn book is making a schedule and sticking to it.

Understanding our 'why' propels our writing. It gives us focus and direction. It cements us as writers – published or not. It unites us as a team with an infinite number of independent working parts. It is the beginning. Now it is up to you to write "The End."

"Show me a hero, and I'll write you a tragedy." -F. Scott Fitzgerald

ATTITUDE IS EVERYTHING

If your life is in trouble or the results you're expecting aren't materializing, change your attitude. It will change your life. And isn't that always our overarching storyline?

Everybody's life contains pain and sorrow, some so tragic it makes you weep just to hear about it. But if sorrow dictates your story, nobody grows. We write about confronting our fears and making changes. The hero/heroine's goal in the beginning of the story is rarely the same goal at the end.

Yet in our real lives, we cling tenaciously to those beliefs which keep us from moving on.

The easiest way to create change is to change our situation, by looking at our problems from a different perspective.

Stop seeking advice from the same people. If you are getting your career advice from those who have neither money nor resources, maybe you should consult another sage.

Maybe you aren't as limited in your skill set as they would have you believe. Maybe the right career is just around the corner, but you're staring straight ahead. My advice to you would be to make a move that cuts into your old beliefs. See the horizon with new eyes.

Some of us fail to act out of fear. What if I make the wrong decision? I would say this – it doesn't matter. You have nothing to lose but the rut you're in. Regardless of whether your choice results in a success or failure, you will have moved to a place where the world looks new.

No one loves change or transition. But thank goodness for them. Without them our lives would be exactly as we imagined in our teen years and then we all would write tragedies.

THE ART OF READING

Reading provides sensory time travel complete with settings, voices, sounds, tastes, scents, hopes and fears. Our job as writers is to evoke emotion. Our readers not only must form a picture of what is happening on the page, but they must be emotionally invested. They must experience your hero/heroine's emotions as their own. Terror, arousal, love, heartbreak, sadness, joy.

When I read stories by a new author, I frequently find that the missing ingredient is the detail that draws the reader into the story. Internally the author sees the scene clearly but hasn't reached the point in his/her writing to convey that information.

Recently I read a story about which I said to the author, "You have talking heads in part of the story." While she was too polite to argue with me, she knew in her heart she did not. Talking heads refers to too much dialogue vs narrative. However, a week later she called to tell me she couldn't believe she'd totally missed that. Nobody wants to hear criticism, but sometimes others see what we miss.

If asked, what is the most important part of a story? Many writers would say conflict. Without conflict, there is no story. But evoking emotion is fundamental to keep our readers turning the pages.

Words provide the transportation that move us to a different world. How many could visualize the world of Harry Potter without benefit of a movie? Or the Civil War South of Scarlett O'Hara? Or the griminess of England during any Charles Dickens' novel?

Does the spoken word do the same? Yes, but in different ways.

Audiobooks conjure photos, but it is easy to get distracted by the nameless voices reading the story. Hearing doesn't always evoke the same emotion from me that reading does. We are put at arm's distance from the emotion by the intermediary reader. However, if I am studying for an exam, I will remember the spoken word longer than the written one, particularly in material where I am not well-grounded. I don't have to experience the thrill of math to learn it.

Reading can transcend a real-life experience. Apparently your brain believes that if one is immersed in a story, the reaction is same as though it happened in real time – which accounts for why many writers are introverts. We don't believe we are missing life. In fact we have a richer set of experiences because we've lived through characters in books.

Reading for pleasure creates different brain waves than reading as an editor and even those are different from the brain waves created by writing. Authors frequently say "I had to shut my internal editor off as I wrote the first draft otherwise I'd never finished."

Reading is one of the most fundamental skills we can teach our children. If a child learns to read he/she can do anything. Sometimes all it takes is the right story at the right time. Like *Harry Potter - Little Women - Captain Underpants* – anything by Dr. Seuss.

In my home my parents decorated with books and everybody read. I am not the embodiment of the well-exercised woman. Sadly I identify more with the King Troll in *Frozen* who has mushrooms growing on his back because my lifestyle is too sedentary. A perfect afternoon would include a good book, a cup of hot chocolate, and a fairy godmother to clean my house, do the laundry and get dinner on the table. We all must find balance. But doing so involves change. What would I have to give up? Giving up or limiting reading might work for some, but not for me. Reading has shaped me into the adult I am today. It has enriched my life and has given me an entire set of friends that comfort me and provide the courage to endure.

"What really knocks me out is a book that, when you're all done reading it, you wish the author that wrote it was a terrific friend of yours and you could call him up on the phone whenever you felt like it. That doesn't happen much, though." – J.D. Salinger

THE IMPORTANCE OF CRAFT

Learning to write a business letter or a newspaper article is not the same thing as structuring and completing a novel. Genre writing is unique in and of itself.

There are those who believe good writing involves plotting and those who believe plotting ruins the story for the author. If the author already knows what is going to happen, the excitement of writing is diminished. Instead of writing that story they will search for another idea.

For every writer, the path is different. If you've got a story struggling to get out, I hope you find the way to get it on paper and I hope you find the time to study craft. But remember this, who would know the name of Mozart if he had only written Symphony No. 1 in E-flat major?

One story does not a career make. But it is the best way to start.

What do readers want? They don't want to trip over grammatical and punctuation errors. We all know that. No one is striving to write poorly. But readers for the most part aren't reading to critique, they are reading because they want a good story.

More than anything else a reader wants to feel emotion. The stories we carry with us are the ones where the character resonated with us. Maybe it wasn't the greatest story ever written, but we read it at exactly the right moment in our lives.

Our goal as writers is to evoke emotion in the reader. When we think of Scarlett O'Hara, Frodo Baggins, or Harry Potter we think of people we've helped overcome obstacles. Through identification with the characters, their fight is also our fight.

We, as writers, have to make the character's quest the best possible challenge. Your character has to face insurmountable odds and be willing to give up everything. If the character holds back, the reader's participation will skid to a halt.

In Titanic, the heroine leapt from the lifeboat onto the sinking ship to save the hero. This resonated with young girls. The heroine gave her all. Older women in the audience, many of whom could author a book, called, "What I Did for Love" may have thought the heroine was a fool, but we weren't the ones who saw the movie fifteen times.

The reader must connect with the characters on page one. This is craft – the heart of a good story. Because evoking emotion is though technique. Angst is drama not emotion. Give your characters a quest they can't refuse with a ticking time bomb in the background. Show the story, don't tell it. Make the setting work. Who can't picture Tara, or Mordor or Hogswart? Done right your work will influence the reader for life. And isn't that why all of us write?

Nancy Brophy
PLOTTING YOUR STORY ARC, WORKBOOK FOR FICTION WRITERS, PLOTTERS AND PANTSERS

STORY
STRUCTURE
PLOTTING

STORY OVERVIEW

Title: _____

Story length: _____

Genre: _____

Novel:	40,000 words +
Novella:	20,000 - 39,900
Novette:	14,000 - 19,900
Short story:	under 13,900

Overall Concept:	
Where I got the idea:	**Trope:**
	Series?
What is the twist? **Why is this story different?**	**What is the overriding theme?**
Date of the idea?	
How long did it take to write?	
Have you checked the storyline requirement of your publisher? **# of words of manuscript**	
Notes:	

EXTERNAL ARC

Title: _____   Genre: _____

Every story must have an external arc which carries the story.
What will be resolved at the end?

What is the problem or the idea behind the story?	Must be quantifiable. The reader must be able to see, touch, feel the goal. The world must be saved, the victim must be rescued, the ark must be recovered.
Why do the Hero and Heroine need each other?	Are the h/h goals going to clash? In genre writing, the h/h must have conflict between them. Otherwise what is keeping them apart? To illustrate this: if the hero is a firefighter, the heroine must be an arsonist. Or if these two people were on a desert island, devoid of external conflict why aren't they together?

Who? Characters
What? Goals
Why? Motivation
Why Not? Conflict
What is the ticking time bomb? A story that can be resolved in 2 years has no urgency. Why must this happen now?
Are there consequences if the story does not get resolved?
Is your antagonist/villain as strong as your protagonist? A super hero needs a super villain. Every fight must be worthy. Whether it is good vs evil (*Harry Potter*), man against nature (*Titanic*) or man vs the supernatural (*Alien*) the reader must be both engaged and worried.

INTERNAL ARC

Title: _____   **Genre:** _____

Every story must have an internal arc which carries the emotional core of the story
In Romance writing, both the hero and heroine must have an individual internal arc.

At the beginning of the story what is the hero's internal (emotional) goal?	How does this change? What does he really want?
At the beginning of the story what is the heroine's internal (emotional) goal?	How does this change? What does the she really want?
Why does the hero want this?	Why does the heroine want this?
What keeps the hero from his goals?	What keeps the heroine from her goals

Remember conflict must be resolved by the characters, not external coincidence. In order for conflict to be sustained throughout the story, thumb screws must be tightened, road blocks constructed and the light at the end of the tunnel, must be an oncoming train.

Weak motivation, weak conflict make a weak story. Motivation must be deeply compelling. The key is to go for fear. What does the character fear to the very bones of his existence? The outer story answers the question what does the hero/heroine want. The inner story answers the question why. Almost all internal motivation is about self-concept and the belief of higher self-worth. Internal conflict is what prevents the character from achieving true self-worth? How does the character feel about himself? Why? What is he terrified to admit?

STORY OUTLINE

Others before me have given an in-depth analysis of story structure.
This is my condensed version. You may want to expand it for your writing.

Ordinary World: Call to Adventure: Cute/meet: Inciting incident: 10% of the story	In genre writing the story must start when the action begins. The ordinary world is sprinkled throughout as backstory. This is the most important part of the book and the hardest to write. Setting up the story line and enticing the reader to continue turning the pages is paramount to becoming a selling author. See the checklist to make sure everything has been included.
Refusal of the call Adding to the fun: Turning Point #1 25% of the story	The call to adventure should upset the status quo of the character's life. Our first instinct is always to refuse the call even if it is as simple a gesture as running one's hand through one's hair and saying, "I don't have the time for this." Most of the time the call is refused by the h/h. In some cases a secondary character could refuse the call for the h/h, such as a mother saying, " You've been sick. You're not well enough to leave." Secondary characters both help the hero/heroine along the journey and thwart their path. A turning point should be significant in the external arc. Put succinctly, the plot should be headed north and take a sudden turn to the east. There are turning points for the internal arc. If you are writing a romance, this means two different emotional turning points. One for the hero and one for the heroine. Frequently one sees the internal arc interwoven with the physical encounters between the h/h. First kiss. First sexual encounter.

STORY OUTLINE

Stuff happens:	The second leg of the book should be a roller coaster of wins and losses in the external arc. The hero and heroine should be moving closer together. Secondary characters reveal secrets. Plot twists. Conflicts mount. Glimpses on what could be and reminders of what each character stands to lose are essential to keep the story flowing. If this portion of the story sags, your story is sunk.
Point of no return: Turning Point #2	The pivotal turning point. The h/h have come too far to go back. The emotional relationship between them has escalated. Frequently illustrated as emotional bond that helps convince the reader this relationship has a chance of a happily ever after. The external arc should also take another sharp turn.
50% of the story	
And you thought it was easy before	Everything that can go wrong does. Our hero and heroine have small victories but the stakes mount and the screws tighten
3rd turning point	In a romance these can all run together, largely because there are so many arcs the author has to wrap up. This should not be easy or obvious. There must be twists, ramped up conflict and the reader must fear that the characters may not make it. Both the hero and the heroine must be prepared to give everything to win.
Black moment	
Climax	Even then the outcome must be in doubt. Frequently in internal arc, a character will decide that the hero or heroine's life is more important and makes plans to sacrifice themselves rather than lose both.
Satisfying ending	In commercial fiction, good must triumph over evil and in romance the final scene must show that the hero/heroine have made a commitment to the other and their relationship will work. They have been through the fire and emerged victorious. Another word of caution, one character – particularly the heroine – cannot give up everything including her home, her dreams, her aspirations and her family for the hero. He must also sacrifice for the survival of the relationship.

"Well, I'm gonna get out of bed every morning... breathe in and out all day long. Then, after a while I won't have to remind myself to get out of bed every morning and breathe in and out... and, then after a while, I won't have to think about how I had it great and perfect for a while."
- Sam Baldwin

Story Arc for Sleepless In Seattle

The general rule for romance writing is that the hero and heroine must meet within the first fifty pages. Sleepless in Seattle is an excellent example of how rules can be broken and the plot still work. The hero/heroine do not meet until the end of the movie, but the audience is fully convinced that the relationship has a good chance of making it. And that there will be a happily ever after for not only the hero and the heroine, but for the hero's son as well.

The movie opens with the funeral of Sam's wife, Maggie in what would be a prologue. The prologue is designed to show in real time rather than in back story where the hero's pain began. To escape the memories, Sam and Jonah, his son move to Seattle to start again.

His goal is to forget and simply survive his life for the sake of his son.

Ordinary World – 1 ½ years later. Christmas.
The heroine, Annie is engaged to Walter. There are spending Christmas with both families and announcing their engagement. Annie's mother tells the story of her own true love and how it was "Magical." Annie doesn't believe in magic or true love.
Sam and Jonah are spending Christmas Eve alone in Seattle.

Call to Adventure.
 Jonah tries to fix his father's unhappiness by calling a radio station and announcing his father needs a new wife. Sam wants to refuse the call but cannot because he wants his son's happiness.

Sam's internal arc is his longing to find another relationship that has magic, but knows he can't because he believes true love only comes along once in a life time.
Annie hears the call. And when Sam talks about the first time he met his wife, both he and Annie say the word 'magic' at the same time.
Whether Annie acknowledges it or not the audience and she understands that Walter is not the right man for her. The relationship lacks the magic needed to last a lifetime.

The unspoken message is that one cannot marry a man she can live with, she must marry a man she can't live without. This is Annie's internal arc.
Secondary characters who move the plot and aid the hero and heroine:
Jonah, Sam's son, initiates phone call.
Movie, An Affair to Remember 1) convinces Annie she must write Sam 2) convinces Becky to mail the letter and 3) convinces Jessica to write to Sam and help Jonah get to New York.
Becky, Annie's friend and boss, who mails the letter and sends Annie to Seattle to investigate writing a story about radio call-in programs.

Even though the hero and heroine never really meet. The external turning points happen in a series of almost meets. Annie hires private detective. Convinced Sam's new girlfriend is a woman he truly likes. He sees her at the airport and is instantly attracted. She watches him play with his son on the beach. They almost meet in the middle of the road, but the most she can manage is 'hello' before she runs away.

The internal arcs show their growing interest in the other.

As Sam begins to date, he chooses Victoria, whom Jonah immediately dislikes. He's read Annie's letter and chooses her because of her mention of baseball.
Jessica, Jonah's friend helps him get to New York.

3rd turning point: Sam plans a weekend with Victoria which produces a fight with his son. Jonah goes to New York without his father's permission to meet Annie at the top of the Empire State Building. Annie is forced to face the truth and break it off with Walter

Black Moment: Sam races to get his son, throwing money in the air to get the taxi ahead of the line. He reaches Jonah just as the building is closing. Annie is not so lucky, but she convinces the guard to let her go up using the movie.

Climax: Sam and Jonah return for his backpack and meet Annie. When they all leave together, Sam takes Annie's hand and it is **"Magic"**.

SCENE GRIDS

SCENE GRID – CALL TO ADVENTURE

SCENE GRID – TURNING POINT TO TURNING POINT

SCENE GRID – TURNING POINT TO TURNING POINT

SCENE GRID – TURNING POINT TO TURNING POINT

SCENE GRID – TURNING POINT TO TURNING POINT

"Dialogue is not just quotation. It is grimaces, pauses, adjustments of blouse buttons, doodles on a napkin, and crossings of legs." – Jerome Stern

When Scenes Don't Work

The hardest scenes to write are transition scenes. Many times they involve traveling or the physical act of getting the characters from one location to another.

There are successful movies I marvel at the writing (and acting). Think about *Speed*. Sandra Bullock spends the entire movie seated behind a bus wheel. In *Apollo 13* the astronauts have no room to move. There are no big sweeping gestures when your entire job is to turn the steering wheel or sit in a captain's chair and occasionally flip a switch.

Yet those movies do not fail to hold my interest because of the emotional chore at the center of the film. Their dialogue is tension-filled.

"We just lost the moon."

"We just put Sir Isaac Newton in the driver's seat."

Or

Jack: It's a game. If he gets the money he wins, if the bus blows up he wins.
Annie: What if you win?
Jack: Then tomorrow we'll play another one.
Annie: But I'm not available to drive tomorrow. Busy.

As the author, if you have written a scene that isn't working, it might lack emotion rather than action. What does the POV character know at the end of the scene that he doesn't know in the beginning? If the purpose of his mission was to land on the moon, how does your character react when that becomes impossible? Changes?

This is the time to reveal secrets, drop a bomb, ratchet the tension and turn the screws. How does h/h react?

Scenes are shorter in today's novels and there are many more chapters per book. This has led to sharper writing and scenes with more punch. Make each scene work toward the end or delete it.

Scene grids are broken into segments divided by the book's turning points. The Call to Adventure has a larger grid because it sets the story and must have enough detail to allow the reader to acclimate to the world you've created.

WORKBOOK CHECKLISTS

FIRST PAGE CHECKLIST

Title:_____

____ Does the first sentence/paragraph grab the reader and pull them into the story?

____ Does the first sentence/paragraph ask a story question?

____ Does the first page immediately evoke emotion? How?

____ Is the main character in jeopardy or a victim of undeserved misfortune?

____ Is the main character likeable? Funny? Nice?

____ Is the main character good at what he/she does?

____ Is the hero heroic? This may not be required for all fiction but for the
        romance writer it is.

____ Is there a definable external goal? What is it?

____ Does the reader know the geographic location of the story?

____ What time of day is it? What time of year? Have you shown it?

____ Does the reader know when the story is set? What century? What year?

____ Does the reader know whose POV begins the first scene?

____ Does your plot combine familiarity with a twist?

____ Have you as the author begun the story in the manner you will continue?
        Or will the reader feel cheated if the story takes an ugly turn?

____ If the first page is part of a prologue, does the prologue reflect where the emotional pain began
        for the hero/heroine?

CALL TO ADVENTURE CHECKLIST

Title:_____

____ What is the compelling reason the hero/heroine accept the call?

____ Many genres, like Romance, must have page one begin with the action in order to draw the readers into the story immediately. As a result the ordinary world is woven in as backstory in small pieces. Does the reader know what happened the day/week the story opened?

____ Is there a ticking time bomb? The Call to Adventure must have an immediate time frame.

____ Is the external arc clear for both the hero and the heroine?

____ Is the external goal quantifiable? Not esoteric. Not will the hero/heroine find love?

____ Is the internal goal clear for both the hero and the heroine?

____ Does the reader understand what the hero must undergo/change to obtain his goal?

____ Is the internal goal/emotional arc clear for the heroine?

____ Does the reader understand what the heroine must undergo/change to obtain his goal?

____ What is keeping the hero from achieving his external goal?

____ What is keeping the heroine from achieving her external goal?

____ Do the h/h have conflict between them that cannot be solved by a conversation?

____ What is keeping the h/h apart beyond external conflict?

____ Does the Call to Adventure answer the question WHO? Characters.

____ Does the Call to Adventure answer the question WHAT? Goals.

____ Does the Call to Adventure answer the question WHY? Motivation.

____ Does the Call to Adventure answer the question HOW? Conflict.

____ Has someone refused the Call to Adventure? Who?

____ What would happen if the call was refused? If life goes on as before, your story lacks urgency, motivation and conflict.

____ In romance a cute meet is optional, but the hero/heroine must meet within 50 pages.

____ Have you as the author laid out the consequences the h/h do not meet their goals?

_____

CONFLICT CHECKLIST

Title:_____

_____ Do the hero and heroine have bone-deep reasons why they cannot get together?

_____ What are the reasons keeping the hero/heroine from reaching their goals?

_____ As the author, are you keeping the conflict sustained throughout the book?

_____ As the author, are you throwing up roadblocks and setbacks, upping the tension/conflict?

_____ Does the conflict appear impossible to overcome? Such as the Titanic is sinking.

_____ Is the conflict solved by the characters, rather than external coincidences?

_____ At the Black Moment when all is lost, are the h/h prepared to give up everything?

_____ Does your plot have a villain, a nemesis or an antagonist?

_____ Is the villain as smart as or smarter than the h/h?

_____ Has your hero/heroine shown true courage in overcoming the challenges?

_____ What can the h/h do at the end of the story, they were unable to do at the beginning?

EDITING CHECKLIST

Title:_____

____ Remove all formatting. Redo. You will eliminate a lot of spacing errors.
____ Print story. Read aloud.
____ Run find for:

> Each character. Make sure their names are spelled correctly. If you have changed their names at any time, run the original name. Make sure all have been changed. Do the same for each location.

> Favorite words: Very, almost, began, tried, turned, that, only, made, finally, nearly, nodded, glanced, groaned, particularly, just, still, back, up, down, really, realized, wondered, pondered, could see, could tell

> For sentences that begin with And or But. Eliminate as many as possible.

> For filter words: Began to, started to, maybe, perhaps, in order to, watched, feel, felt, thought

> For it. Define whatever it is. Watch for sentences that begin with: it was or there was.

> For that. Eliminate as many as possible.

____ Read the first paragraph of every scene.

____ Read the last paragraph. Does it ask a story question or end on a hook. Is there a reason for the Reader to continue turning the pages.

____ Make sure your chapters are numbered correctly.

____ At the beginning of each scene, have you grounded the reader. Does he/she know who, where, what, why, how? Is the POV established and identified in the first paragraph?

____ What are your characters wearing in each scene?

____ Have you incorporated hearing, smelling, touching, tastes and sight into each scene?

____ Rewrite:

> Sentences that end in a preposition, such as: about, above, across, after, against, as, at, before, by, for, from, in, inside, into, near, of, on, onto, over, since, through, to, toward, under, upon with, within, without

Action verbs that convey nothing, such as: move. How did the character move? Did he glide, stalk, slink, stomp. Watch is bad, because it also shows no action. Make sure you are not overusing pushed, pulled, glanced, reached, looked, stood, grabbed, stepped, little, long

Clichés. Not only the well-known ones. But ones that every novel of that genre contains. In romance every novel I read contains a variation on the character smiled, but the smile didn't reach his eyes.

Repetitious sentence construction. (Pronoun – to be verbs are common) He was, she had.

Dangling body parts. Her eyes were glued to his chest.

To be verb followed by action verb with –ing construction. He was trying to dance. Either he danced or he didn't.

Adverbs – learn to hate them. Most are identified by –ly. She was really pretty.

_____ Write in active voice. Eliminate passive.

_____ Balance narrative with dialogue.

_____ Avoid changing POV in a scene.

_____ If you've already shown, don't tell it.

_____ Buy a thesaurus. Use a variety of words.

_____ After you've done all this, hire a copy editor who will find more.

"Description begins in the writer's imagination, but should finish in the reader's." -Steven King

LIGHTS, CAMERA, ACTION CHECK LIST

Is the action happening in real time? Does the reader experience the action with the character? Have you shown the emotion rather than told it?

Carol felt angry v. Carol's eyes narrowed and her lips tightened into a grim line.

Have you used visceral clues of the character's feelings or reactions to the action?

Sweat beaded on her forehead and under her breasts.
Her palms itched. She shuddered.

Details, Details, Details:

If the heroine is crawling across a battlefield what is on the ground? Is it rough or smooth? Are there twigs or rocks? Are there fallen soldiers? Is it daylight? Twilight? Pitch black?

Which shows the story better?

Jake crossed the barroom and slapped money on the poker table.

Jake stormed across the planked floor, the clicking of his heels audible despite the loud music and rowdy laughter. The game was well underway when Jake slapped two twenties and a ten on the wooden table.

Have you used color, size, shape, smell, scent, sound, taste and texture?

Have you used active verbs?

Called, ran, hopped, captured, hunted

Have you used action verbs with precise meanings?

Did your character walk? Or did he amble? Slink? Jog? Take a jaunty stroll?

Are you telling readers how to feel or letting them discover it for themselves?

In a totally unexpected move, the man jumped from the car into the river.
Or
The leaves of the bushes shuddered. Zack crouched, waiting.

Have you used the exact words a character spoke? Are you using action tags to illustrate the characterization?

"Halt!" Grant's voice carried the weight of his ten years as a police officer.

Do your words paint pictures? Imitate sounds?

The sky thundered. Lightening crackled.

"Half my life is an act of revision." - John Irving

Back Story Checklist

Not all stories include the information I need to know. For example, how did a non-magical King and Queen produce a daughter, Elsa who generates an entire frozen kingdom by merely waving her hands? Why did Red Riding Hood's mother let her journey into the woods alone? What promise did Aunt Petunia make to her sister, Lily about raising Harry Potter?

The other side of the coin is the info dump which is more prevalent in new writers. Generally the big flaw is: too much, too soon. Learning to weave backstory into a novel in pieces in an important part of storytelling. The author gives glimpses, dribbles in info. It's a form of flirting. One flashes an ankle, bares a shoulder before disappearing behind ostrich fans.

Backstory halts the forward action of the story. People have secrets, dribbling backstory into a novel isn't about the mundane. It's about trust, guilt, censure and fear.

We are observant beings who discover things about other people in small increments. The same thing should hold true in your stories. If you feel the reader must know every detail, write a prequel.

Timing, timing, timing. Rushing the backstory will ruin your story.

Cut, cut, cut. Will your story survive without the backstory? I read once that writing backstory feels like story telling but it's not. Story telling moves the story forward.

Checklist:

No backstory in Chapter One.

Is the backstory dribbled in, not one big dump?

Does the other character need the information? Why?

Have you, as the author, cut it to the absolute minimum?

Is the back story relevant?

Is the information tied to some type of action?

"You don't write about the horrors of war. No. You write about a kid's burnt socks lying in the road." Richard Price

THE ART OF DIALOGUE

Whether the story is about a woman's journey to fame, "Hello Gorgeous," or a woman's failure to grasp the direction her life has taken, "I have always depended on the kindness of strangers," well-written dialogue plays a major role in viewers' connection with those on the page or on the screen.

Villains intimidate through words. "I'll get you, my pretty, and your little dog too!" made most of us quake in our boots when we were nine. Or thirty-five. "No wire hangers, ever!"

Dialogue, even without tags, says everything about your characters. A man who says, "You're quite the little bitch," is a different, calmer character from the one who screams, "You bitch!" And yet, the words are almost the same.

Without dialogue, where would we be in the art of flirting? That fluttering fan-thing would get old quickly. But a woman who says, "You know how to whistle, don't you, Steve? You just put your lips together and blow" wants exactly the same thing as the woman who says "La-dee-da, la-dee-da." They just represent different characters. And we wonder why men are confused. Would you say yes to a man who uses a pickup line? "Your eyes are as blue as my toilet water at home." No?

Writing is very different from speech. To convey verbal communication through the written word, speakers use contractions and they do not necessarily speak in full sentences. Dialogue must reflect tension. Tension is not conflict. Tension is emotion. When you meet your mother-in-law for the first time, there is tension. When you meet your ex and his new wife, there is tension. When you do a presentation at work, there is tension.

Life is full of pacing dialogue techniques such as: Interruptions. Silences. Repetition. Short, choppy answers. Long winded explanations. The girl who can't shut up. The guy who communicates in grunts.

There are different schools of thought on how to do dialects. Many times an accent can be implied through arranging words differently. "Rome is beautiful, is it not?" "Well, lassie, your mum's been a missing you, I've been thinking." Cumbersome dialects are best left unwritten. Most importantly, dialogue should advance the story and reflect character.

"I love writing. I love the swirl and swing of words as they tangle with human emotions."
-James Michener

Layering Emotion

An idea tickles the back of the mind. A minor character in a movie causes you to wonder about his backstory. A concept arrives at your doorstep though some mystical connection you don't even begin to understand. It doesn't matter how it starts. The point is this idea/concept/person would make a great novel. You rub your hands in glee like a greedy banker.

In your mind's eye you can see the story unfold. Of course there would be a movie made. Acclaim. Wealth. JK Rowling, Margaret Mitchell, Steven King, George RR Martin move over. A villa in Tuscany? Why not?

You sit at your desk. Heck, you've got a couple of weeks. Like the Holy Grail, this idea is a shining beacon drawing you closer. It won't take any time at all to drop the words onto the page. In fact this story will practically write itself.

Six months later the pages no longer glow. In fact there is a griminess to them that produces dread. Some days you reread what you've written and are proud. Other days, you wonder how you graduated from high school.

Finally, your spirits lift as you write the words, "the end", break out the champagne, and dance around the room in your snoopy pajamas.

"Nice first draft" is a comment you don't want to hear, but every story needs editing. And it is through editing that the author layers in the missing elements. Now you are deepening the story with color, atmosphere, noise and emotion.

Each season holds scents, sounds, tastes, temperature, sights and touch. Snuggling in one's furs is a giddy sensation while trailing one's fingers in the cool water from the stream smacks of a person in love. Setting can be another character in the story. Think of a hobbit hole or the shrieking shack as examples in literature.

In your own life, remember a time when a significant emotional event took place. As you think back on it, startlingly clear details will emerge. For example if the event took place in a Laundromat the smell of detergent and bleach would be omnipresent. Can you still recall the color of paint of the principal's office, the first time you were in trouble?

Answer the questions on your character's grid. Now go back to your story and deepen the characters' nuances, add quirks and visceral reactions. Does every scene contain the senses? Is your breath visible on a cold day? If you are standing in a field in West Texas can you hear the clicking sound of pump jacks across the road? Does the smoke from the barbeque pit make your eyes sting, but the succulent smell of cooking meat make your mouth water as it draw you closer? Does the hair on your arms rise when you hear a noise in a dark room?

What does your character know intuitively? We sum up people and situations every day with only a glance. Body language speaks volumes. Barbara Sue twirling a finger through a curl tells us something different than seeing Aunt Helen slumped against the porch pillar.

When Captain America opens the pocket watch with the photo of the 1940's girlfriend, what does that tell us?

Emotions can be interpreted in different ways. In *Cinderella*, the stepmother plays the piano while one daughter sings and the other plays the flute. The girls get into a scrabble and the mothers urges calmness. The Cinderella knocks on the door, the stepmother's face contorts into rage as she slams her fingers onto the piano keys, making a jarring note and screams that Cinderella knows never to interrupt the music lesson. Personally, I attributed the stepmother's reaction to menopause, the movie went with wicked.

Bugs, spiders, snakes creep people out, as do certain types of people. A spider I can kill, but a cobweb serves as a reminder I haven't cleaned. Adding guilt to all my other internal expectations.

Movies use music to forewarn us about the seemingly innocent barn. In your story are birds are chirping in the trees or are vultures circling in the distance? Is it a light cleansing summer rain or a torrential downpour that has the gullies overflowing?

Delores Umbridge made pink a sinister color. And don't even discuss the importance of showering after you've seen *Psycho*. Is there anybody who doesn't fear the power of the ring? "*One ring to rule them all. One rule to find them. One ring to bring them all and in the darkness bind them...*'

In *Titanic* every time the heroine wanted to burst through the confines of her position, her clothes played a restrictive role. It is not until she removes them that she is able to leave her old life behind.

Layering is texturing the story. Details draw readers. Tapping into universal emotions allows readers to remember the story long after they've put down the book. It is emotion that connects authors and readers. And it is emotion that will help purchase that villa in Tuscany.

"Every good story deserves to be embellished." Gandalf

LOCATION, LOCATION, LOCATION

In our race to be published, one can easily forget that craft is the cornerstone of this industry. If the reader doesn't identify with the characters, your battle is lost. And that identification has to be established on page one.

Here's the problem: you publish a mediocre story or you publish a good story, but not a great story. Your reader yawns and puts the book down. Even if your next story is better, you may not get that reader back.

One of the most overlooked areas for this quest is in the details of the location. I know America has become homogenized and that you could take a snap shot of a strip mall on a tree-lined street in almost any town and everybody would recognize it as their own. But if you're setting a story in Any Town, USA no one will care.

Think of any small town, maybe the one your grandparents grew up in, then think of Mayberry or Lake Woebegone. Can you picture the difference? Chicago vs LA? Paris vs Shanghai? Tara vs Manderley?

Each town, each location, must be unique. Some authors refer to it as another character in the story. It can be menacing or welcoming, but it must represent something identifiable to the reader.

In the movie, *Silver Streak*, after the train tore through the station and ended up in a gift shop, the metal face of the engine was ripped open in a ghastly grin. The train was an excellent example of another character in the story.

Characters are larger than life. They don't choose to live in average places. To sell the initial concept of Pixar, the filmmakers did a short of a mother desk lamp with a child desk lamp and a ball. When the ball deflated and the child desk lamp was broken hearted, so were you. Pixar understood conveying emotion through inanimate objects. It is why their movies have resonated with the public and why, to this day, Pixar still uses the desk lamp as part of their image.

Could the stories you love, the ones on your keeper-shelves, been just as good set in another location? Is that like asking if the Flintstones could have lived on The Ponderosa, instead of Bedrock?

CHARACTER DEVELOPMENT

"Dreams are the touchstones of our characters." — Henry David Thoreau

ADDING DIMENSION TO YOUR CHARACTERS

Character motivation hinges on self-esteem. People are multi-dimensional. The question is how to portray that in novels. I prefer to write about dysfunctional families – crazy parents and imperfect siblings. Emotions so closely interwoven that loving doesn't eliminate killing. Many of us do not want to admit that it is our families who help form us into the adult we become. Imagine the difference in the personality of a woman who is the daughter of June and Ward Cleaver vs the daughter of Dan and Roseanne Connor.

Family is important, so important, in fact, that a lot of writers make the hero/heroine orphans. As a writer, you can't simply state 'the parents were insane' – you have to show it. Erratic personalities are more fun to write, but also have a tendency to take over every scene. The heroine throws up her hands in disgust and walks off. The hero/heroine never come together, and the romance author (who really liked the crazy one better than the heroine anyway) has to shelve that story under the bed. At least, that's how it happens in my life.

Your characters must come to you with invisible wounds. As writers, we must flesh out those ancient injuries and expose them to the world. By putting a face to the wound, we make it human and lovable.

Characters without wounds have no story. Personalities shape us, but social and economic factors are heavy contributors.

What if your hero/heroine's family was wealthy? Not just a few bucks in the bank, but owned so many homes/private islands/retreats they'd lost count of the number. A common fantasy we harbor, involves slipping into the life of the idle rich, but most of us would have no idea how to handle the money or the situation. Like lottery winners, we'd have to declare bankruptcy within a few years.

If one were truly rich, how could a stranger overcome your character's inability to trust? How big a factor is the money in a relationship? Would the other person have to be even richer to prove their sincerity? Can one really fall in love with a rich man as easily as a poor one? In the regency period, a marriage based upon an exchange of goods and services. An arrangement with status would allow a rich American, to marry a poor but upper crust, titled, aristocrat who found the American crass, but needed her money. Oh, the sacrifice.

What if the life your characters lived turned out to be a lie? Like the children of Bernie Madoff? Or Aldrich Ames? What if everything they valued – respectability, honesty, financial stability, position within the community – disappeared overnight because of someone else's actions?

Imagine your hero/heroine's entire life lived under the shadow of an evil relative? Not family secret evil, but villainy known by all – scorned and hated solely because of a last name? Living in Germany with the last name of Goebbels or Hess cannot be popular even decades after the end of WWII.

Physical appeal plays an important role. Most of us fall in the middle of the looks continuum, not hunchback of Notre Dame ugly and not Sleeping Beauty beautiful. But if strangers wrote sonnets to your appearance, would anyone ever see you for who you truly were?

I spend a lot of time fantasizing about how a new story should begin. In my mind, that which is not yet written is shiny and perfect. I write the Call to Adventure without knowing anything about the character's backstory. In doing so, I meet the characters as one would in a real life drama. Like an onion they reveal themselves a layer at a time through their words and actions. Their true natures play out on the page.

These are characters who will be with me for a long journey and there have been times when I've kicked them out of the car (or stuffed them under the bed) because they haven't convinced me their story is worth the endeavour.

But they are a sneaky lot. Not happy being under the bed, they will creep into another story pretending to be a sidekick, but actually biding their time until they have revealed themselves to be complex enough that it becomes impossible to do anything but put them front and center, while exposing their wounds to all.

Even our superhero must have vulnerabilities. Kryptonite can be fatal, but finding a person who can see beyond the mask is close to impossible. Whether your character is fictional or real, the truth is simple. It is hard to find someone who truly loves and understands us, as it is popular to say – warts and all.

HERO

"A hero is someone who has given his or her life to something bigger than oneself."
-Joseph Campbell

WHAT MAKES A HERO HEROIC?

All people have the capacity for bravery and acting beyond their comfort level. Some do it as a matter of routine. Others force themselves to act when no one can or will. When we think of heroes, we tend to focus on certain qualities including:

Accountability, accuracy, acumen altruism bravery, calm, caring, confidence, courage, dedication, determination, discernment, honesty, independence, insight, intelligence, loyalty, modesty, patience, power. Reliability, resilience, resourcefulness, respect, responsibility, strength, valor and wisdom

Who has been a hero in your life?

_____

_____

What qualities made that person heroic?

_____

_____

What careers are best suited for a heroic hero?

_____

_____

With some careers it is easy to identify heroic aspects, but in order to avoid the generic hero, what special qualities does your hero possess?

_____

_____

What situations might make an ordinary person heroic?

_____

This page has been left blank for photos or drawings of your hero.

THE HERO CHARACTERISTICS

Title _____

Hero

Name:	Age:	Nickname: Why:
Height:	Weight:	Tattoos
Hair color	Eye color	
Education:	Military service:	
Occupation:	Previous jobs:	
Divorced:	Widowed:	
Religion:	Higher Power:	
Hobbies:	Quirks:	
Core beliefs:		
Lives where:	Why:	
Accent:		
Rich:	Poor:	
How does he feel about money?		
What is his personal motto?		
Physical flaws/body image:		
Glasses:	Favorite body feature:	
Parents:	Brothers and sisters:	
Children:	Does he want them?	

THE HERO CHARACTERISTICS

Hero

Social status:	
Feelings about family:	
Hair - long or short:	Style:
Does he resemble an actor? Which actor?	
Makeup:	Jewelry:
What does he fear the most?	
What sets him apart?	
Has he had a serious relationship? What happened?	
How important is sex? Into kink?	
What does he fantasize about?	
Does he have a special strength or skill?	
Team player:	Lone wolf:
Does he see himself as the one in charge?	
What is his vulnerability?	
What is his fear?	

THE HERO CHARACTERISTICS

Hero

Day Job:
Is he good at it?
What kind of car?

Style of dress:	Home décor:
Dreams:	Fantasy career:

How do others see him?

The Hero Characteristics

What does the hero want?	Why?
Why doesn't he have it?	How is he going to get it?
Who is standing in his way?	Who is helping him get it?

Has your hero been in a previous book? What do you already know?
What about him attracts the heroine?
What do you as the author know about her that the reader doesn't?
Why is he attracted to the heroine?

HEROINE

"I was not rescued by a prince; I was the administrator of my own rescue." - Elizabeth Gilbert

TODAY'S HEROINE IS NOT CINDERELLA

When I first announced to my family that I was writing fiction, they were thrilled. But when I added the words 'romance novels' my brother asked incredulously, "You're writing bodice rippers?" And while the rest of my family did not second his opinion publicly, privately they may have thought it.

The phrase 'bodice ripper' just won't die. When I hear it, the one thing I know for sure is the person using it hasn't read a romance novel – ever. Today's novels are not the ones your mother read. And the major difference is the heroine.

We still have the historical, although the pirate book has lost favor. But one day someone will write a good pirate story and suddenly they'll be hot again. But we will never go back to the virgin heroine whose first encounter with sex was to lose the 'no, no, no' fight – a woman portrayed as a victim of men, society and Puritanism.

How did those novels ever gain acceptance? Two things. One was a backlash reaction to the free love generation of the late 60's and early 70's. The paradigm shift from 'you can touch my left breast, but not my right' morality to 'sex is great with whomever you want anytime you want' was more difficult for a lot of women than reported. And the second was that as authors writing about sex, we utilize knowledge from our own histories. If the writers were at least thirty years of age, their experience came from an earlier time. A time when pre-marital relationships were okay if the woman didn't really consent.

Women have changed. On television, we've gone from June Cleaver, housewife with pearls, to working single gal, Mary Tyler Moore. Claire Huxtable was a mother and a lawyer, married to a doctor (how proud her parents must have been) to Carrie Bradshaw a sex columnist (what do you suppose her parents thought?).

In real life we've gone from Eleanor Roosevelt to Jacqueline Kennedy. From Margaret Thatcher to Hillary Clinton and Sarah Palin. Romance novels have kept pace with the times. The new heroine is never a victim and she doesn't need a man to save her. In fact a lot of times a man is in her way. These women are tough. They're raising kids on their own. They work, some own businesses. Many have impressive kick-ass skills. Every one of them has attitude and spirit.

Men have to work harder now because their duties have morphed from meal ticket and protector to partner, lover and friend.

Many of today's romance authors have had previous careers as lawyers or medical researchers or scientists. As women have grown and changed so has the industry, offering sub-genres from the supernatural to modern contemporary. From historical to futurist. From erotic to chaste. And everything in between.

And yet we still have romance novels. In fact the percentage of their market share has increased. Maybe because it is escapist literature. Maybe because we all need something that has a guaranteed happy ending. Or maybe because through it all, love endures. Either way, I'm proud to be romance writer.

This page has been left blank for photos or drawings of your heroine.

The Heroine Characteristics

Title _____

Heroine

Name:		Age:		Nickname: Why:
Height:	Weight:		Tattoos:	
Hair color	Eye color			

Education:		Military service:
Occupation:		Previous jobs:
Divorced:		Widowed:
Religion:		Higher Power:
Hobbies:		Quirks:
Core beliefs:		
Lives where:		Why:
Accent:		
Rich:		Poor:
How does she feel about money?		
What is her personal motto?		
Physical flaws:		

Glasses:	Favorite body feature:
Scars:	Body image:
Parents:	Brothers and sisters:

The Heroine Characteristics

Heroine	Children:	Does she want them?
	Social status:	
	Feelings about family:	
	Hair - long or short:	Style:
	Does she resemble an actor? Which actor?	
	Makeup:	Jewelry:
	What does she fear the most?	
	What sets her apart?	
	Has she had a serious relationship? What happened?	
	How important is sex? Into kink?	
	What does she fantasize about?	
	Does she have a special strength or skill?	
	Team player:	Lone wolf:
	Does she see herself as the one in charge?	
	What is her vulnerability?	

The Heroine Characteristics

Heroine

What is her fear?	
What does she dream about?	
What kind of car does she drive?	
Style of dress:	**Home décor:**
Day job:	**Good at it:**
How do others see her?	

The Heroine Characteristics

What does the heroine want?	**Why?**
Why doesn't she have it?	**How is she going to get it?**
Who is standing in her way?	**Who is helping her get it?**

Has your heroine been in a previous book? What do you already know?
What about her attracts the hero?
What do you as the author know about him that the reader doesn't?
Why is she attracted to the hero?

THE VILLAIN, THE NEMESIS, THE ANTAGONIST

This page has been left blank for photos or drawings of your antagonist

The Villain, Nemesis, Antagonist Characteristics

Title: _____

Villain

Name:		Age:	Nickname: Why:
Height:		Weight:	
			Tattoos
Hair color		Eye color	

Education:	Military service:
Occupation:	Previous jobs:
Divorced:	Widowed:
Religion:	Higher Power:
Hobbies:	Quirks:
Core beliefs:	
Lives where:	Why:
Accent:	
Rich:	Poor:
How does he/she feel about money?	
What is his/her personal motto?	
Physical flaws:	

Glasses:	Favorite body feature:
Scars:	Body image:
Parents:	Brothers and sisters:

The Villain, Nemesis, Antagonist Characteristics

Children:	Does he/she want them?
Social status:	
Feelings about family:	
Hair - long or short:	Style:
Does he/she resemble an actor? Which actor?	
Makeup:	Jewelry:
What does he/she fear the most?	
What sets his/her apart?	
Has he/she had a serious relationship? What happened?	
How important is sex? Into kink?	
What does he/she fantasize about?	
Does he/she have a special strength or skill?	
Team player:	Lone wolf:
Is he/she in charge?	
What is his/her vulnerability?	

The Villain, Nemesis, Antagonist Characteristics

What is his/her fear?	
What does he/she dream about?	
What kind of car does he/she drive?	

Style of dress:	Home décor:
Day job:	Good at it:

How do others see him/her?

The Villain, Nemesis, Antagonist Characteristics

What does the villain want?	Why?
Why doesn't he have it?	How is he/she going to get it? How far is he/she willing to go?
Who stands in the way?	Who is helping her/him?

Has this character been in previous books? What does the reader know?

What makes the character unforgettable? This character has the best role in the book. He/she should be larger than life. One word of caution. If you are writing a series and plan to redeem this character and elevate him/her to a protagonist in another story. Structure his/her motivation carefully.

Villains must also have a strong arc and their motivation must tap into a universal theme. In *Harry Potter*, Voldemort is the villain who can destroy the world, but surveys have shown the character that the readers hated the most was Delores Umbridge because she taps into The Universal theme of cruelty. Most have experienced a situation where someone in a position of power takes advantage of their role with petty cruelty.

Notes:

"I will not ask for forgiveness. What I have done is unforgivable. I was so lost in hatred and revenge." - Maleficent

REDEEMING THE ANTAGONIST

An antagonist (sometimes known as a dark hero) can be a protagonist in another book given sufficient motivation. An excellent example of a recent movie would be *Maleficent*. In *Sleeping Beauty* as the antagonist she is the self-proclaimed Mistress of All Evil. *Maleficent* tells the tale from the point of view of Aurora (Sleeping Beauty).

Ordinary world – The story opens with the unseen voice of a narrator setting the scene. She informs us that two kingdoms lay side-by-side but there is great hostility between them. The human kingdom is run by a greedy king while the Moors (the magical kingdom) has no ruler because all the magical folk trust each other. She informs us that a prophesy states the two kingdoms can only unite with the aid a great hero - or an evil villain.

As a happy powerful fairy, Maleficent is a young girl living in a tree in the Moors. She is able to mend growing things and is friends to the magical people and the animals in the forest. Even as a child she is seen as a leader. She encounters a human boy, named Stefan and shows him life in the magical kingdom including allowing him to fly by holding on to her feet. Stefan points out the human castle and states his goal is to live there one day. Their friendship grows into something more. On her sixteenth birthday he presents her with true love's kiss, but his affection is overshadowed by his ambitions in the human world. Stefan refuses the lure of happiness with Maleficent and does not return to the magical realm.

<u>**Initial Goal**</u> – Maleficent protects the Moors. Flying through the clouds to feel the sun on her face gives her happiness and a sense of well-being. Her wings represent trust, freedom, power and all things she values. Stefan's true goal is not only to live in the castle but become a man of worth and power.

<u>**Characters:**</u> The audience (reader) identifies with the heroine because she has power but is kind and becomes a victim of undeserved misfortune. Stefan, too, appears as a boy who has heroic qualities and undeserved misfortune. (He lives in a barn, but is ambitious and throws away one of his few possessions– an iron ring – when it cause pain to the heroine.)

Call To Adventure – Stefan's desire for power deepens as he ages. The greedy King wants the Moors under his control. He wages war only to be overpowered by Maleficent and injured. On his death bed, the King offers the throne and his daughter to the man who can defeat the faery. Stefan, a servant of the King, seizes this opportunity. He revisits the Moors with the plan to deceive Maleficent, drug her, kill her and bring the proof to the King. Unable to commit the murder, he takes her wings instead. As he leaves he hears her devastating anguish and turns his back on his "true love" in exchange for being crowned king. Note: karma is used frequently as a subtext.

<u>New Goal</u> – The loss of the wings equals the loss of her ability to fly, the loss of her trust and the loss of her humanity. Her judgment is clouded by her grief and her kingdom turns dark. Flowers wither. Happiness flees. Her hair which has been worn down and free is now bound in a tight cap sometimes made of snake skin.

Adding to the fun – Weakened she fashions a powerful walking stick and makes her way into the mountains to be alone. A crow chances upon her and when she pushes him away, he falls under the net of a woodsman planning to beat him to death. Maleficent changes him into a man, saving his life. In exchange the crow, Diaval, vows to become her servant.

Diaval serves as her informant. Stefan has been crowned king. The realization that Stefan betrayed her to gain the throne devastates Maleficent and sends into a spiral of vengeance and anger. In retaliation, she forms a dark oppressive kingdom with Diaval as her one companion and confidant. Diaval spies on the King and informs Maleficent that King Stefan plans a christening for his newborn daughter, Aurora.

1st Turning Point - Bent on revenge, Maleficent arrives uninvited and states the newborn will grow in grace and beauty, loved by all who know her. Then adds she will prick her finger on her sixteenth birthday and sleep forever. Stefan is forced to beg for his daughter in front of the entire court, in return she offers a caveat. The curse can be broken – and she paused and stares as Stefan - by true love's kiss. She rejoices in her cleverness. This is the perfect trap because the one lesson Stefan taught her was that true love isn't real.

Since Stefan uses love as a manipulative device, he also realizes that his daughter will never awaken. But Stefan's goal of power interferes with his concern for his family. He is bent on revenge for the humiliation he has suffered by having to beg and lose face in front of his kingdom. Oh, yeah and he's angry about the curse on his daughter thing, too.

Stuff Happens - Stefan sends Aurora to live with three incompetent pixies until one day after her sixteenth birthday. He orders all spinning wheels in the kingdom broken and burned, hiding them in the deepest dungeon in the castle. At the same time he stays behind the castle walls and wages war, sending out his armies to find and kill Maleficent, but she, too, builds walls, surrounding the Moors with an impenetrable wall of thorns.

Despite her initial dislike for Princess Aurora. Maleficent takes responsibility for the girl when the careless pixies fall short. As a toddler, Aurora comes upon Maleficent in the woods and demands to be held. Instead of being fearful, the child is curious about her horns and has no problems cuddling up to her. After that Maleficent watches over her from afar. <u>**This is the first emotional turning point.**</u>

Point of No Return: When Aurora is fifteen, Maleficent allows her to see the Moors while she watches from the woods. The child encourages her to come out. Much to the shock of Maleficent, Aurora announced she is not afraid and recognizes the older woman as her "faerie godmother" aware that she has been watched over all her life. Maleficent's shadow is always with her.

Maleficent grows to love the princess – perhaps because of her curse that she will be loved by all who meet her and makes a serious attempt to revoke the curse, but cannot, having invoked magic that ensured no power on Earth can change her words. **2nd emotional turning point** Stefan sinks into madness. He can't visit his dying wife because his true obsession is with Maleficent and spends time conversing with her wings being held captive in a cage.

Aurora visits the Moors and like Maleficent before her, she, too, is adored by the animals and the magical beings. Much of Maleficent's happy childhood is resurrected. We see glimpses of Maleficent changing. When the toad-like creatures throw mud. Some accidently hits Maleficent and creatures tremble, Diaval laughs and instead of getting revenge on the toad-like creatures, she throws mud on Diaval.

3rd Turning Point: On the day before Aurora's birthday, Maleficent, in an effort to thwart the curse and reverse her own magic, suggests the girl move to the Moors, far away from any spindles. Aurora agrees, leaving to tell the pixies.

As Aurora practices confronting her guardians to announced her departure, she meets Prince Phillip, and the two are smitten with each other, but have little opportunity to build a relationship. Aside from the fact the prince looks like one of the boys in One Direction, it is the first time we see Aurora visibly shaken by someone around her.

The pixies, who still haven't learned to cook, inform Aurora of her parentage and why she can't marry some idle guy wandering around the forest. She is a princess under an evil spell and name Maleficent as the wicked faery. Aurora confronts "her faerie godmother" before running to her father. **The 3rd emotional turning point**

And you thought it was easy before: Stefan isn't particularly overjoyed to see his daughter as she is interfering with his plans for revenge. He locks Aurora away for her safety.

However, the dark magic cannot be undone. It draws the princess to the dungeon where she pricks her finger on a magical spinning wheel. Immediately she falls into a deep sleep. Intent on saving her, Maleficent abducts Phillip and infiltrates Stefan's castle to have him kiss Aurora and break the curse. Diaval warns of a trap and is told he can stay behind. He refuses, grumbling about how she needs him and a little recognition of that fact would be appreciated.

Beginning of the external arc climax - Phillip's romantic, but chaste (dry) kiss has no effect, as physical attraction may be the first step toward love, but deep love takes time and commitment. The pixies are annoyed by the Prince's ineptitude and send him away.

Maleficent apologizes to Aurora and swears no harm will come to her, kissing her forehead. This maternal affection/love breaks the curse and causes Aurora to awaken. True love as we learn comes in many forms.

Black Moment – (characters must give their all) -Aurora forgives her and they attempt to flee the castle, but Stefan's revenge plan is in play. An iron net (similar to the net that held Diaval) traps Maleficent who fights back by transforming Diaval into a dragon. As she has done to him, Diaval lifts the net off her, but is harnessed by the soldiers.

Circled by his men eager for revenge, Stefan beats Maleficent with an iron chain. Before he can kill her, her wings, freed from his chamber by Aurora, reattach themselves. With her wings back, Maleficent overpowers Stefan and breaks free. He becomes trapped in the iron chain still wrapped around her feet. As she flees she carries him to a high tower. Unlike their childhood play, this flight is not filled with mirth and joy. Her emotions are riding high, but we can see she has learned the importance of not letting her anger rule her. Instead of killing him, she stops herself and declares their feud over.

Stefan, however, has learned nothing. He attacks her when her back is turned, but plummets off the tower to his death. As she descends the shadow of her wings covers him in death just as it has in life.

Happily Ever After - Aurora is crowned queen of the human and faerie realms by Maleficent, who once again wears her hair long and free. The two kingdoms are unified by Aurora with Phillip at her side. The narrator then reveals her own identity as an older Princess Aurora. (Satisfying ending – Good triumphs over evil). The narrator also notes that uniting the kingdom took someone who was not just a hero or a villain, but both.

Realized Goal: Maleficent flies into sky and regains her happiness. Kingdoms are united. True love comes in many forms.

Characters, Locations, Identifying Marks

If you are writing a series this list will save time and effort.

CHARACTER NAMES		AGE	JOB	EYES	HAIR		NICKNAME	LOCATION

Characters, Locations, Identifying Marks

CHARACTER NAMES		AGE	JOB	EYES	HAIR		NICKNAME	LOCATION

RESEARCH

This page is left blank for you to add research photos or information pertinent to your story.

"If there's a book you really want to read, but it hasn't been written yet, then you must write it." -Toni Morrison

WRITING AS A CAREER

I don't know anyone who thinks they can't write a novel. And not a mid-list book either, but a best seller. If only they had more time. But they have a family, a job, soccer practice, dinner to put on the table, and vacations to take. It's a shame really, because they could be the next Stephen King, Dan Brown or JK Rowling. If only life hadn't gotten in the way.

There are others who have started a manuscript, but floundered. They received negative feedback from a friend, spouse or contest. They sagged. They folded. They lacked enough passion to rally back and fight. No doubt it was harder than they thought. No doubt it sounded better in their mind than on paper. No doubt another career called their name.

I envy the perfectionists. Chapter one, scene one is written, and rewritten, and rewritten again. Every comma is perfect. Each word resounds with meaning upon meaning. When they die, they have achieved twelve perfect pages. Others believe a first draft is a final draft. No need to edit or rewrite. Women will weep; men will envy. Any editor who would dare to reject such a masterpiece is an idiot.

One of my favorite stories is about the English teacher who finally decided she'd made her point that good writing is in the re-writing when a student left a sign on her door one day. "Should I kill myself? All that lies before me is suffering. Dying would rid me of that pain…." Hamlet Act 3, Scene 1 First Draft.

We have got the excuses. The hardest book to finish is the one never started. Writing does not come from muses or the girls in the basement. Writing is a career that requires earnest dedication and continual work. You can find 150 things to do on your computer each day besides write.

There are blogs to read and blogs to write. There is email to answer and games to play. But no matter how much I lie to myself, that isn't writing.

Setting up a website, marketing or designing my cover isn't writing either. Although I do admire authors like JD Salinger who write one perfect book and become a recluse. So far, I'm struggling with making that plan a reality.

I'm finding my process. It's an excuse I've used more often than not. But here's the ugly little secret I've learned. Each book is a new process. I've written fast and slow, at home and on the road. I've plotted and made storyboards. But as long as I can find other things to do, I put off the hard work of getting the story onto the page. I fight writer's block constantly.

Here's my best idea. While thinking about my characters and the scene I need to write, I find a favorite author and a scene of a similar purpose. I start typing their words while thinking about my characters. Within a couple of sentences, my words take over. By the time the book is finished, I've edited and changed every sentence so many times, the other author's words are gone.

My problems do not come from external sources. I battle my inner self who, given an opportunity, would drink scotch and eat chocolate all day. As the Pogo cartoon character once said, "We have met the enemy and he is us."

I know there are people out there who don't struggle. I hear about them all the time. But the funny thing, is I've never met one. Most of the writers I know suffer, suffer, suffer. And they want to tell you all about it, because the rules of suffering are like the rules of surgery. Minor surgery is on someone else.

In fact, that might make a good novel. Why don't I just sit down and whip that out, right now? In the process, I'll open a vein, because that is what novel-writing really is, giving your life force to your story.

When Do You Plan To Write?

Calendar

_____Month_

Sun	Mon	Tue	Wed	Thu	Fri	Sat

Writing Goals

a record of your plan and a record of your action

Mon	Tues	Weds	Thur	Fri	Sat	Sun	Total	planned	achieved

"I used to be Snow White, but I drifted." - Mae West

WHAT A ROMANCE WRITER CAN TELL YOU ABOUT REAL LIFE

No one offers a course in really important life lessons. They'll remind you about rules from kindergarten. How important it is to play nice with others or not run with scissors. They'll teach you how to meditate to reduce stress, which you'll need from the burden of always playing nice with others. But once the sh*t hits the proverbial fan, you're on your own. While you may think a romance writer lives a life of perpetual joy, we do occasionally have moments that aren't bliss-filled.

Here are a few of the lessons I've learned.

Life Lesson One: When to Lie

If a man in a dark suit comes to your office and says: "Are you (fill in your name)?

Your response should be, "Absolutely not. I'm here to meet with her for an appointment but she's stood me up. Good luck waiting for her." And then leave as quickly as possible. Because telling the truth will inevitably get you another sentence you will hate.

"I'm from the IRS." Or "You've been served."

Life Lesson Two: When to Dial 911

If you arrive home to find your house filled with dark smoke, do not stop. Drive to Starbucks and drink a long cup of coffee or get a pedicure. Any time-killer you can think of because a smoke-damage fire is worse than losing everything. (Trust me.)

Life Lesson Three: Work is Work

Do not drink with your fellow co-workers. Do not use the Christmas party as a time to unwind. Do not assume just because you hate your boss, that everyone else feels the same way. And I shouldn't even have to say this one, but if you are out on the town with co-workers, do not use this opportunity to score with a hooker or make a drug connection. Believe it or not, I have seen people fired for all of the above. And if you do any of the above and get away with it, do not post it on your Facebook page. See Lesson Four.

Life Lesson Four: Living Large on Your Social Network

My mother used to say, "Never put anything in writing you will have to defend in court." This is a rule society has gotten away from and it needs to be brought back home. I am shocked at what people put in writing. Not just on YouTube or Facebook, but in emails. Once that missive has left your computer, the world will have the opportunity to read it. Consider your thoughts carefully.

Life Lesson Five: Treasure the Real Things

It is easy in this day and age to put your marriage/family on a back-burner. Kids, work, dinner and house payments conspire to suck the life out of your day. You're tired and cross. No, you don't want sex. You don't even want to cuddle. All you want is a few minutes alone. Is that too much to ask?

If you knew you would die in two days, what changes would you make? And isn't that the true lesson a romance writer teaches us? Make time to tell your family how much they mean to you. Make time to find sweeter words and a kinder voice. Make time to really learn how to play nice with others.

EXAMPLE

HELL ON THE HEART – CALL TO ADVENTURE

Chapter One

Armadillo Creek, Texas

With one hand gripping the slender branch, Cezi Romney stretched until only her fingers clung to the rough bark as she peered through the thick leaves of the sycamore tree to the ground far below.

Her breath tumbled out in short gasps from the quick scramble up the ladder and across the bathroom roof only to discover she had limited her options. A tree limb no more substantial than a PVC pipe extended almost to the roof line, so with a small leap, she tiptoed across the branch, muttering both swear words and protection spells each step of the way.

After stashing her purse and shoes in a lower notch of the branches, she climbed another ten or so feet skyward into a tree that did not welcome her intrusion.

Cezi concentrated on breathing deeper, slower and quieter. Nothing could be done about the deafening noise of her heart as it careened through her chest crashing into her ribs. How could she not think of herself as a fool when this scenario was the ideal fodder for an intelligence community training video.

What Not To Do
starring
Czigany Romney

FBI recruits would take turns pointing out exactly where she went wrong.

Not that she was FBI or any one of the other alphabet soup groups that protected the country. Government law-enforcement agencies had stringent requirements in hiring that precluded an asthmatic, twenty-six-year-old, high school dropout whose idea of a clever hiding place was an enclosed playground.

As a nearly-licensed Private Investigator who worked for the family business, she followed cheating husbands. And wasn't that the complete opposite of being a CSI?

So how had she ended up on a moonlit night, twenty-five feet above the ground, hiding from a man, good-looking enough to rival Hollywood's leading men and so scary she used every ounce of self-survival instinct to protect herself?

"Oh, little thief. Come out, come out wherever you are." The deep voice turned the singsong chant sinister.

His words annoyed her in the way a buzzing wasp would make her want to shake and squirm, but they also kept her tightly focused.

Waiting him out wasn't working. For the past ten minutes, he'd circled, his shoes striking the concrete surrounding the wood-chip playground as he rattled the locked bathroom doors and checked the hard plastic swings, climbing equipment and slides to locate her hiding spot.

"Are you playing games?" His inflection dropped to a lower pitch, more sensual. He planned to seduce her out of hiding? "You like games? I know a lot of games we can play."

She bet he did, but his intent was more serious than consulting a bankruptcy attorney when she could no longer afford to own Boardwalk and Park Place.

Why wouldn't he just go away? Then she could laugh about this whole adventure and her life would return to normal. The evening hadn't been a total loss. She'd figured out the top five rules she'd incorporate in the future, should this situation ever arise again.

Rule number five. NEVER get distracted from the job paying your salary. Following cheating spouses bored her, but she hadn't ended up being hounded by a man who appeared to have a handle on crazy.

Rule number four. Good looks did not equal good intentions. Cain McIntosh, the man stalking below, was hands-down gorgeous and she came from a family of hunky guys. Fifteen annoying male cousins had women falling at their feet, but none could compete with this guy in the pretty-boy department. Yet, every one of them she'd trust with her life. This man made her sphincter tighten with fear.

"Come out, little thief, while you can. If I find you first, I'm going to have to punish you. Come out now, and I'll make sure we both enjoy it."

The truth of her mother's words struck home. *If temptation were easy to resist, who would care?*

Like a melody his words floated to her. "Ah-h. So you like the chase. What happens when you get caught? Is being tied up one of your secret fantasies?"

The squeaking sound of metal scrapping against metal made her pause. The swings? How long could checking the playground equipment take? Coming here was the worst idea she'd ever had.

Rule number three. Learn self-defense. Being manhandled in public was mortifying. Worse, it made her relinquish control. In a family of dominating men, she'd learned to stand her ground in verbal spats. But this wasn't a man who gave a rip about how well she argued. He reverted to the age-old male theory - might makes right.

"Are you touching yourself, little thief? Longing to be turned over my knee and spanked? You're being very naughty. You want to be punished, don't you?"

No, she didn't.

Rule number two. Don't be greedy. He had pissed her off when he'd grabbed her breast. So she'd lifted his wallet, cell phone and watch. She'd resorted to petty theft when she only needed his wallet.

"You know what's going to happen when I find you?" The door handle of the bathroom rattled as though it had magically unlocked itself since he'd tried three minutes earlier. "I'm going to spread your legs and lap up all of your sweet cream until you scream my name. You'll like that. Coming over and over again. Being at my mercy as I torture orgasm after orgasm from you."

Cezi clutched her knees together. His words were intended to be sexy, but they failed. She wasn't a woman men bothered to seduce. For one thing her male cousins didn't let anyone get close, but the real reason was she didn't inspire men to reckless statements.

Should she just go down and give him back his stuff? He hadn't done anything to merit her stealing from him. He didn't appear mad now. Just horny. She shifted her weight grabbing a thick twig for support. The snapping of the wood as the thin branch gave way echoed in the night air.

Cezi froze. Had he heard the noise over the hum of the nearby air conditioners, the scrunching sounds of tires on blacktop, or the continuous chirping of crickets. Unable to see him, she worried he stood directly under the tree peering into the branches.

Powerful bikes roared. Harleys? Headed this way? She bit her lower lip, her lipstick long gone. The engines ground to a halt nearby. Cezi leaned over, clinging to the branches to locate Cain's position.

The crunching sound of leather-soled shoes on woodchips alerted her to his presence. Parting the leaves she searched the ground below her, seeing him as he strode toward the gate. Was he leaving?

Her sigh of relief was premature. Two men, looking like Hell's Angel recruits, stepped inside the playground. Cain wasn't going anywhere; he'd called for backup. And that brought home her number one rule. Never ignore her inner voice that told her to be afraid. Be very, very afraid.

"Heard you had a problem."

Cain shushed them and spoke in a low tone. She couldn't distinguish his words. He gestured around the area and didn't point toward the tree, which made her breath come easier. His men scanned the playground without leaving their position.

Cain's posturing was a lie. The fact he'd called in re-enforcements upped her anxiety. Why was he so concerned about a few personal items? Granted the cash in his wallet, thirteen hundred and twelve dollars, was more money than she ever had, but had he been robbed, would he have tracked the muggers as intently? Despite the cool night air, she wiped sweat off her upper lip and her forehead.

One of the men reached around his back and handed a Cain a gun. The blued barrel glinted off the street light before disappearing into the waistband. Both newcomers snapped on headgear. Night vision goggles?

Cezi's stomach rolled and she swallowed back the bitter taste of bile. These guys weren't fooling around. Hell, they'd be able to tell where she was even in the trees from the heat her body gave off. She wouldn't have to come down. They could shoot her out of the tree.

Her own idiocy trapped her. No way out, but up. And that offered little enticement other than a farther drop. She untangled her body from the branch and tentatively placed her foot on the closest climb, grateful for her tomboy childhood.

Three men armed with night goggles and weapons to bring her down and she didn't have so much as a nail file.

The gate creaked and clanged closed again. Shifting her position, she pushed another branch aside to see. The younger blond man from the bar, the second best-looking guy she'd ever seen stood at the entrance - Cain's partner in crime. Although she wasn't quite sure what the crime was.

Prior to seeing the limo, the blond man started this mess by getting Ellie Parker drunk. Where had he been and where was Ellie? What had they done with the limo?

Cain mumbled and the blond man snarled back. "Yeah, I took care of it."

Even from the distance of the tree she could see these men weren't BFF. *Took care of it? Took care of what?*

A loud crash startled her. Her body jerked. Had one arm not been draped around a substantial branch, she'd have tumbled toward the earth. She peered through the tangle of branches below her.

"Hey!" Cain whirled from his position by the fence and paced toward the bathroom. As he crossed under the light she struggled not to gasp at the ugliness in his flawless features now distorted in anger. "Quiet! We don't want locals coming to see what's going on."

"Just checking the bathrooms," a gruff voice replied.

"Use your brain, numb nuts." Cain lowered his voice. If she hadn't been directly above them, the words wouldn't have reached her. "No windows. Padlocked from the outside. How the hell do you expect her to be inside? Kicking the hinges off the door leaves a trail."

Cezi's lungs seized. What had been merely fear escalated into panic. She rested her weight against the thickest branch and strove to get a full breath as she dug in her pocket for her inhaler.

Sweat dampened the hair on her neck and around her face. Breathing took precedence over everything else. If they heard the gust of the inhaler, it didn't matter. Without air in her lungs, she'd pass out and fall to her death anyway.

Her hands and arms stung, chaffed and scratched from handling the rough bark and twigs. She struggled to calm her thoughts and waited for the medication to take effect. The men hadn't been drawn to her position, but the one consistent thought she couldn't seem to vanquish was that of a large, flashing neon bulls-eye on her back.

Gradually the oxygen permeated her lungs, allowing the laborious climb to continue. Each handhold required weaving through the leaves and twigs, while every inch she gained in height was paid for with scratches and jabs from sharp protrusions.

Reaching the highest place with enough cover to offer protection, she snuggled into the crotch of two sturdy limbs. Pressed against the trunk so tight she became one with the branch as she attempted to make herself as small as possible. Two things had always held true for her – her family and luck. Tonight she needed both. Luck the searchers might mistake any heat source as animal rather than human this high in the tree and her family to rescue her.

The bark bit into her skin, but she forced her back flat. Dismissing any thought of pain, she shielded the light from her phone with the fabric from her skirt and texted Uncle Luca about her predicament.

That done. Nothing else remained but to wait for the Cavalry. Her tangled hair caught on a branch and pulled when she turned her head. To pass the time, she combed out the trapped twigs and leaves and braided two long plaits.

Chapter Two

Cain checked and rechecked every inch of the fence line. Without an underground hole, she couldn't have left the area. His pilots, Peter and Paul climbed to the bathroom roof and scanned the area. Cain clenched his teeth, knowing the other three men were probably winking and nudging each other, delighting in his problems. In five years Cain had never called for help. His decisions in the field had never been questioned. His team. His call. His actions. These bastards wouldn't even have jobs if it weren't for him.

His stolen watch added to his exasperation. His ten thousand dollar Cartier watch. The watch he'd chosen when he turned his back on his old life. No longer was he the one dumped by some whore who'd traded up for a better meal ticket.

At least a dozen times he'd bit his tongue to keep from lashing out in anger. When was the last time, some little bimbo had given him this much trouble?

He would have his revenge. Once they had her. If Eli hadn't gotten the other girl drunk, they'd be out of here by now. But Cain had been pushed to give the boy a chance. Eli screwed up big-time, which forced them to dump the blonde.

The petite brunette wasn't his first choice, or even his second, but his evening was ruined and now the dumb bitch would learn there was a price to be paid.

Unlike the other girls he'd taken back to Mexico, he planned to keep her all to himself. He might even take a couple of weeks off, so she could see what happened when she dared to defy him. The mere thought of her screams made him harder than he'd been in months. Turning toward the fence, he readjusted his pants, easing the pressure of the zipper. Once he bored of her, he'd give her to the others. This girl wouldn't be protected from damage. When Herod finished with her, there wouldn't be enough left to sell.

A smile crept to his face before he sobered and reminded himself to stay in character, but silently he promised over and over. She would be his - whether the little slut wanted it or not.

He breathed deeply, pushing a calmness he didn't feel into his voice. "Little thief, you're starting to wear my patience. Come out now or things will be much worse for you."

"Cain," Peter whispered from the top of the bathrooms. "We've found her."

"Where?"

The chunky pilot pointed upward.

She'd climbed a bloody tree? Who the hell was she? Sheena, queen of the jungle? "Go get her."

"Honey, you need to come down. Now." Peter scrambled across the limb to the trunk. The branch dipped precariously with the man's weight. "Get me a flashlight."

Eli jogged to the bikes to return with a large nine-volt battery powered light. Paul tossed it to Peter. The bright beam filtered through the leaves to the top of the tree.

"There you are. C'mon down now."

#

What was with these guys and the sexy crooning? Even the new, armed guy sounded like he enjoyed this game. In fact, she was probably the only one not anticipating the outcome.

Uncle Luca, where are you?

She needed a different backup plan, but damned if she knew what it was. Terror gripped her mind and twisted her stomach.

Climbing down, she took her time, doing more shifting and futzing than actual descending. "Do I need to come get you?" The charm left his voice.

"No. I'm coming."

"Well, pick it up, honey. I don't want to be here all night."

"Up's easier than down."

He didn't bother to reply. Instead he called to his companions, "Here, catch." The shoes and purse she'd tucked into crook of a lower branch landed on the bathroom roof with a thud.

"Hey, Cain. Here's your watch."

"What about the phone and wallet?"

"She must have them with her."

She did. Tucked between her breasts at an awkward angle. Her broken strap, thanks to Cain's ruthless manhandling, left one breast exposed unless her hand held it. "If I throw you the rest of his stuff, will you go away and leave me alone?" she asked the man in the tree.

He guffawed in disbelief. "You're way too late for that. Cain already has a special plan for you."

Cezi suspected as much. "That's no incentive to come down."

"This isn't a negotiation, girl. Either you come down or I'm coming up. And if I have to jerk you out of the tree, it won't bother me, even if you drop, say twenty or thirty feet."

She inched down the tree, taking more time than needed.

An impatient voice called from the ground, "What's taking so long?"

"Stalling," Her guard reported.

"I'm not. This is harder than it looks." But even with every delaying tactic she could employ, eventually she reached the point where he could get a hard grip on her.

Once his thick arm was wrapped around her, he pushed her toward the branch that crossed to the roof. "You first." Waiting for her on the other side was another man whose response was an eerie grin distorted by the neon vapors of the streetlight. Of all the men he was the least attractive with two missing teeth and a nose spread across most of face.

"C'mon, baby, I'll catch you."

The thought that she'd crossed to the tree in heels indicated how stressed she'd been. In bare feet it was a serious balancing act. As soon as she reached the flat roof, the man snatched the protruding wallet and the cell phone from her chest. "Anything else in there?"

"Nothing worth mentioning." Words too true for comfort.

"Catch," he said to someone below, dropping the wallet and phone over the edge.

"Lower her down."

"C'mere, Princess."

Cezi shook her head and backed toward the ladder attached to the rear of the building. "I can climb."

The guard from the tree grabbed her arm. With a hard jerk, he tugged her toward the edge where the other man stood. "You've been enough trouble already."

The men captured her hands and lowered her over the side. Her bodice gapped open, exposing her left breast. Everybody snickered, but Cezi.

Cain glared at her. His dark brown eyes glittered with a red tint. She clenched her flaying knees together as the men above lowered her to the ground. Fetid swamp water, sweat and expensive cologne assaulted her nose.

Evil has a smell of its own. Her mother's words swirled in her brain.

"That's far enough." He lifted her stiff petticoat and peered underneath. "The way you've pushed my buttons tonight, I'm surprised your panties aren't white."

He twisted her exposed nipple, making her bite her lip to keep from crying out. "Too late for a show of bravery. By the time I'm through, you'll be begging for mercy."

Do not wheeze. Any weakness will be exploited.

Cain gestured to the men holding her hands to lower her further. Once her feet touched the ground, he yanked her hands behind her and bound them together with what Cezi suspected was one of her stockings. She fisted her hands in an attempt to bulk up her wrists as much as possible, hoping he would tie her loosely, giving her room to wiggle out. No such luck. The binding continued to chafe when she relaxed her muscles.

The heavy hand he placed on her shoulder pushed downward until she knelt in front of him. The tree's shadow had covered her, but now her face was illuminated. She blinked her eyes to adjust to the light.

Kneeling at their feet, insulted her. Insulted her gypsy heritage, but her legs had been ready to buckle. She wasn't sure standing under her own power was possible.

Fear mingled with nausea had her stomach doing aerobics. Her teeth clenched until her jaw ached, muscles bunched in knots, eyes glared until dry. His jeering response convinced her she looked about as tough as the grinning Kool Aid pitcher.

"Do you have something you want to say to me?" He circled her in what appeared to be a slow victory lap.

Cezi hesitated. Yeah, she had a lot she wanted to say, but every word would further inflame the situation. She swallowed her pride and attempted humble. "I'm sorry."

He laughed, a loud abrasive sound. "That's real nice, but those aren't the words I want to hear."

They weren't? She shifted. Small stones dug into her knees. Out of the corner of her eye the men from the roof sauntered around the edge of the building, each sporting wide grins.

Cain grabbed her chin and yanked it up so she stared into his smiling face. Of all the things for her to notice, his teeth were very white and straight.

All the better to eat you with. The terror Little Red Riding Hood felt had certainly been glossed over.

"Don't know what I want? Let's start with a little action." He jerked open his belt buckle. On her knees it was impossible not to know what was coming next.

"What's with the braids?" He wrapped them around his fist and twisted. Her head followed the direction he pulled. "A handle? Something for me to hold on to?" Tears stung her eyes and she tried to focus on something besides the pain. The noise that came from him wasn't humorous, although she suspected he meant it to be. "How old are you?" He unzipped his slacks with his free hand.

Cezi sucked in a breath and squeezed her eyes tight, waiting. Her brain froze, unable to form a coherent thought let alone a plan of escape.

Words of salvation cut through the quiet night. "She'll be eighteen on her next birthday."

Her lungs dumped their load in one loud, wheezing gasp. The voice of the happiest man she knew, Uncle Luca, held an unsuspected menace that sent a shiver running down her back.

"If I were you, buddy, I'd be real careful what you pull out of your pants. Messing with an underage girl in this state is a felony."

Cain released her hair as he straightened to face his opponent.

Cezi leaned forward to see if Luca was alone. Oh, hell, he'd brought every male in the family. At least fifteen guys stood together. And each prominently displayed a gun and an attitude.

The weighty hand returned to her shoulder. "Friends of yours?" She bobbed her head, not trusting herself to speak. "Well, aren't you the lucky-"

"Are you okay, Peata?" Uncle Luca interrupted.

She nodded again unable to form words.

"Your girl stole from me," Cain said.

Hysterical laughter bubbled up inside her. Did he think it would offend her family to claim she was a pickpocket? These were the ones who taught her.

"I returned everything." The words sounded less defiant than she meant them.

Uncle Luca shrugged. "Well, there you go. Unless you want to press charges, I'd say we're done here. Untie her and help her up."

While the younger man eased the knots, the roof man produced her shoes from his pockets and dropped them to the ground, followed by her purse. Cezi didn't bother to put them on; she scooped them up and made a beeline for safety behind the front wall of her defense.

What would her family do? Would they kick Cain's ass? Her cousins tussled all the time, but she never seen them fight for real. She twisted her neck trying to see between the barrier of males standing between her and Cain's group.

Rolf, Luca's middle son, dropped back to quiz her, "you okay?"

"Fine." She managed through gritted teeth.

"Right." He grabbed her shoulders. The warmth of Rolf's hands rubbing her shoulders anchored her. "That's why your head's shaking no."

She pursed her lips to glare at him, but immediately refocused her attention back on Uncle Luca, waiting for his next words. Cain would know the terror she'd felt.

Luca's head jerked toward the gate, so quick she almost missed it. *What? This was it?*

"Let's go." The soft command came from someone standing in front of her.

Rolf's hand on her shoulder guided her with a gentle, but firm push toward the gate. She looked over her shoulder at Rolf, holding a question in her eyes.

"Get in the car," he murmured. "We'll talk later." The group surrounded her, crowded her

between the larger men to form a protective barrier as they marched to the gate.

Dammit, they'd let the bastard win. With one quick glance back, she saw a cruel smile

etch Cain's features.

"We're not through, little thief," he hollered after her. "Not by a long shot. Keep watching

over your shoulder, because one day soon, I'll be there to collect what's mine."

Chapter Three

Washington, DC

It wasn't rain. It was a deluge. Fifteen minutes earlier, gray clouds skated across the sky. Without warning, the heavens opened and drenched the unsuspecting commuters winding their way through bumper-to-bumper traffic in the nation's capital.

John Stillwater straightened his cream colored tie as he eyed his soggy image in the glass door of the insurance company. Prerequisite dark suit, wingtips, briefcase and a corporate haircut supported his image as a life insurance agent for Family Protection Insurance.

Nothing could be done about his face. He bore the marks of a warrior not only in his eyes, but a series of scars spider-webbed the left side of body from his eyebrow to his chest, compliments of the 2004 Madrid train bombings.

His shoes sank into the thick gray carpeting as he skirted the empty front counter where a woman waited, drumming her fingers on the glossy wood, shifting her weight from stiletto to stiletto.

"Are you an agent?" She demanded as he attempted to slide by unnoticed.

Dammit. He braced himself. Her sharp voice laced with a strong sense of entitlement made his skin crawl. From experience he suspected the woman's bravado would collapse once he turned. Gasps and repugnant looks of horror were rare, but women with children crossed the street to avoid him.

He pivoted on his heel, schooled his tone to east coast professional. "What can I do for you, ma'am?"

He'd guessed right. The woman took a step backwards and clamped her jaw shut. John waited while she fought for words.

"File a claim," she stammered.

He purposely looked at the large clock on the wall, turning his head so that his scars were more visible. "Our office doesn't open for another fifteen minutes. If you'll have a seat, someone will be with you shortly."

The woman backed until a chair appeared behind her knees and collapsed into it as Miranda, the pleasantly round gray-haired receptionist came through the front door, flapping her umbrella to leave as much of the rain outside as possible.

"Good, you're here. This woman needs assistance." He both gestured and smiled, to imitate a true-to-life insurance agent, both actions foreign and clumsy. He preferred an economy of movement. A life of military stealth was hard to reverse.

The receptionist gave him amused acknowledgement as she played out her role, allowing him to escape. He ducked behind the partition that separated the lobby from the serene offices.

The decor soothed. Subtle earth tones and rich woods blended to create harmony or as he secretly suspected a barrier from the chaos that reigned one floor below. At a solid door in the far corner marked private, he punched in a code. A series of metallic clicks followed by a hollow-core thump indicated the tumblers had slid into place. The door opened and he stepped into a small stark-white alcove.

Placing his palm against a pad and his eye against a scanner, the machines verified his identity.

"Good morning, Agent Stillwater," the monotone female computer voice droned as the interior door sprung open to reveal an almost sound-less elevator that took him to the basement level. "Welcome back."

He didn't answer. The noise sensitive computer recorded any response. Another alcove.

Another door and finally he was in the FBPA office. Automatically, he reached up to loosen his tie and unbutton his collar.

"You're back." D'Sean Lassiter leapt to his feet in a sleek cat-like move. On more than one occasion his agile body and quick wits proved essential to their survival. "Was Minnesota as bad as you thought?"

"Montana." Stillwater corrected absently. "Worse actually. Who's here?"

Gray metal desks, savaged from some defunct military installation were crammed together, hemmed in by white walls lacking any ornamentation save that of the United States flag and a framed photo of the President. But despite the no-frills décor, the Federal Bureau of the Protection of Americans or the FBPA served its function well while not beholden to any overseer group other than as a direct adjunct to the President himself with the proviso that the last thing the country needed was one more secret government agency working independently of others.

Information sharing was essential. As a result, the small, tight, handpicked group operated hand-in-hand with both FBI and Homeland Security.

"Everybody except Twylla and Skeet," D'Sean said. "She's stuck in traffic, but should roll in any minute and he's doing the weekly curtsy at Quantico."

Stillwater studied the black man as he spoke. Something was different. "You shaved your head. Cornrows got old?"

D'Sean ran long tapered fingers over his newly shorn head. "What'd you think?"

Stillwater shrugged. What'd he think? He thought his partner of ten years looked like his partner, but without hair. "It's not what I think that matters. Do women think you are still 'lickable'?" He raised his eyebrows in amusement as he quoted one of the many barflies who'd lusted after D'Sean.

The black man laughed. Combined with his smooth looks, many were fooled into doubting his ability as a warrior. Stillwater knew different. No one else could be trusted to have his back, and he was confident D'Sean believed the same. But that didn't mean their relationship didn't include a heaping helping of trash talk. While the rest of the team approached carefully, D'Sean lived to annoy.

"What's not to love, Tonto?"

Stillwater grunted, refusing to give in to the taunt. Tonto. His Indian heritage was a fact, but he was nobody's sidekick. And he was nobody's whelp. "I bet Shantell could answer that better than me."

Shantell was a crazy woman, the kind that flocked to Lassiter like dust to computers. The black man sported two superficial gunshot wounds from a wild night in Chicago when she'd chased him down a hotel corridor firing a Saturday-Night-Special. He'd taken a load of shit from the team over that incident. Even more after it became public knowledge that he'd been buck-naked at the time.

D'Sean scowled. Direct hit. John smiled for the first time since his return from Montana.

Lassiter wasn't one to go down without a fight. "Your day's coming, Tonto. Some hot little mama will take you in hand and you'll never know what hit you. She won't be like those other women you choose, so eager to please." His fingers fluttered under his chin and he batted his eyes.

John snorted, confident in his retort. "Never. Women I see know the rules. They're welcome to come home with me at night as long as they're gone in the morning."

D'Sean shifted his shoulders as though warding off an invisible hand as he scoffed in disbelief. "I can feel it in my bones. Hundred bucks says it happens before Christmas."

Almost seven months? Piece of cake. "You're on. Gather everyone in the conference room in…" he glanced at his watch, "twenty-seven minutes."

He heard Lassiter's amused chuckle as he sauntered back into the bullpen to spread the word. Stillwater dropped the file folders onto his desk and closed his office door.

Winning the bet would be a snap. This case promised to be his undoing. As a healthy male, he liked women. And women liked him back, despite his scarred face or in some cases because of it. But recently he couldn't talk to a woman without evaluating what each of her actions or reactions would get her if he hadn't been one of the good guys. It'd be a miracle if he managed another date before Christmas.

In thirty-four years, he'd seen more than his fair share of human misery and cruelty. Every time he closed his eyes, the shattered faces of the young girls he interviewed danced before him. Good thing sleep was overrated.

The girls in Montana were the lucky ones. They'd been rescued. Family and friends waited to welcome them home and help put their lives back together. How many other parents waited for word on their missing daughters?

As he concentrated on entering details from the Montana trip into his computer, D'Sean opened his door a second time and poked his head inside.

"What does the schedule look like for this week?" D'Sean attention was focused on the cellphone glued to his ear and for a brief moment, John wasn't sure the question was directed to him. His fingers poised above the keyboard hung in midair while he waited to see if D'Sean needed him to respond.

"It's not an issue. I can get there," Lassiter spoke into the phone addressing the caller on the other end. Concern and intimacy flowed through his voice. This was a personal call.

John returned his eyes to the monitor and resumed working, giving his partner privacy that hadn't been requested.

"Are you sure?" Lassiter asked after several minutes of silence. John glanced up and D'Sean shook his head mouthing 'never mind' as he disappeared into the hallway, pulling the office door closed behind him.

Stillwater immediately dismissed the call from his mind. If Lassiter wanted to share the details, he'd volunteer them.

The conference room was a misnomer. It was the only place that had enough chairs for the team to gather and compile data. John chose the chair at the far end of the rectangular cherry wood table, a discard from the upstairs Insurance office.

RJ "Ciggy" Reynolds, computer geek and demo expert, pulled up a chair next to him, flipped it around and threw a leg over the seat. "Judging by your expression, I'd say you didn't get what you wanted." His freckled moon-shaped face belied his concern. Unlike the rest of the team, Ciggy actually looked the part of an insurance agent despite the fact he'd shed his jacket and tie.

Stillwater ran a hand through his hair. "I did and I didn't. We have a break through, but the situation is much more pervasive than we imagined." He nodded to each of the others as they trickled through the door and took seats.

D'Sean, the last to arrive, settled on the opposite side. "So what do we know?" Around the table the three men and one woman leaned in closer for a detailed report.

John shook his head. "Nothing good. My info confirms all our suspicions."

The group groaned.

He opened the top file. "Becca George," he flashed her driver's license photo from three years earlier, "just turned sixteen. In the middle of the day, two men, one with a television camera knocked on her door in Shreveport, Louisiana with a huge bouquet of balloons. Told her she'd won a ten thousand dollar shopping spree at a local mall from a contest she didn't remember entering. A limo was to take her to the television station for the public announcement. Her parents were already on their way to meet her at the station. The sixteen year old didn't even hesitate. Once she was in the back seat of the limo, she doesn't remember another thing until she woke up naked, cuffed to a bed in a strange house."

He pulled another photo from the file folder. "Here is what she looks like today. Nineteen. Haggard. Underfed. Scars, bruises and broken bones decorate her body with the addition of intimate piercings and a branding that I can't even imagine how painful it must have been."

He grit his teeth to keep his anger from spewing forth. The others at the table, hardened men and woman, all ex-military, who had seen both combat and suffering, looked shocked as he recited the facts.

He opened the second file folder and passed another photograph. A typed bundle of pages held the next girl's story. Stillwater didn't refer to his notes. Each story was imprinted in his memory.

"Courtney Shaffer and her best friend, Sarah Pickens were looking for a night of adventure before they headed off to college the following week. A limo driver, waiting for his boss, convinced them to try a three-way in the back of the limo. It was all fun and games until the boss showed up. The limo driver scrambled out to explain the situation. The last thing Courtney remembers is the limo motor being turned on. She never saw her friend Sarah again. I've checked the records in Clearwater, Florida. Neither girl has been heard from in twenty-seven months."

More photos changed hands. At the end of the table, Dare posted the pictures on the whiteboard and carefully printed their names and abduction date underneath.

"The third girl was a college student, Missy Harding. She left a campus party about midnight. Two men standing beside a black limo were arguing over a map. She offered to help, and since they were going in the same direction she accepted a ride home."

"Oh, man," Ciggy mumbled under his breath, loud enough John heard.

"That's not the end. At the party she and her boyfriend had a fight, which was why she left the party alone. He was tried, convicted and hanged himself in prison."

The room was silent while the man absorbed the damage done to both families.

Dare directed their attention back to the situation at hand. "How are they subduing the girls?"

"I'm assuming the limo is rigged with some sort of gas that's being piped in. Probably activated by a lever from the driver's seat. None of the girls could remember smelling or hearing anything unusual. Most limos have a window between the driver and the passengers. Closed and properly sealed, anybody in the front seat wouldn't feel the effects of the gas."

"How'd they escape?" Ciggy asked.

"Fluke accident. The fact they're still alive is a damn miracle."

Twylla jotted notes on a legal pad. Without looking up, she asked, "Do the girls remember anything else?"

"Yeah. All the girls were kept prisoner in large house for two-to-three weeks. Each girl described an attractive bedroom with a private bath."

"That doesn't sound much like hostages."

"Get this, all the girls could identify at least six men by name. Misty thinks they were aliases because they were all Biblical names. No masks were worn and according to each of the girls, each man was polite."

"Stockholm syndrome?"

"No. The men used an enforcer. So if the girls cried, complained or refused to perform in any way, Herod showed up. The only reprieve from the bedroom was when Herod introduced them to his little torture chamber in the basement. The girls were terrified of Herod until they spent some time in the Middle East where staying alive became their first priority."

"Could they pinpoint the desert location?"

"No. No one spoke English, at least not to them. They learned through gesturing and pain."

Frustration ricocheted through the room. "So what is our break-through here? Other than the black limo, do we know anything else?"

"Yes."

Twylla's lips curled in a rueful smile. "Finally, some good news."

Stillwater shook his head. "There is no good news. I requested a computer search in the Fed's central crime database on how many missing persons involved any mention of a black limo. It came up with four hundred and thirty-seven cases from coast to coast. Then I had them search for the general MO. Young girls, unlikely runaways, nobody ever recovered and found an additional thirteen-hundred-seventy-three cases."

The room remained silent as each tallied the numbers.

"Ciggy, look for a pattern in the location sites. The rest of us need to categorize the different MOs and look for similarities other than a black limo."

His phone rang. He glanced at the screen - Skeet Monaghan, public face of the FBPA. "Stillwater."

"A call came for the FBI. They think the case is ours. Armadillo Creek, Texas reported a murder."

He clicked on the speaker, so the team could hear the call. "A murder?"

His disembodied voice echoed in the room. "One witness indicated a black limo was involved."

Ciggy frowned. "Are our guys escalating? Or is this a coincidence?"

"Coincidence? Since when do we believe in coincidence?" Skeet asked. Without waiting for an agreement, he added. "Two things. One, Armadillo Creek hasn't invited help and two, the sheriff's office discounts the witness."

The first didn't bother John. The advantage of not-being FBI meant they didn't need to be invited in. An unreliable witness could be tantamount to wasted effort. "Why?"

"No idea. Do you want me to tell them we'll check it out?"

"Yeah." Every person in the room glanced at their watch.

No doubt Skeet was doing the same thing. "I can meet you at the plane in forty-five minutes."

John shook his head. "No. Doesn't seem solid enough. Lassiter and I'll go down and see if it's worth bringing everyone in." Stillwater clicked off the phone and was surprised to see his partner wince. What was his problem?

To Ciggy, he said, "Find out what you can. Get us a complete workup."

Ciggy gathered his notes and rose to hit the banks of computers in his office. "Armadillo Creek, Texas. Never heard of it."

"Me, either. Find that out first." Both men walked toward the door. As he passed Lassiter, he said. "Wheels up in thirty minutes." Automatically, he buttoned the collar on his shirt and tightened his tie. Time to go to work.

STORY OVERVIEW

Title: Hell On The Heart

Story length: 80000 word

Genre: Romantic suspense

Novel: **40,000 words**

Overall Concept:
Two men, flip sides of one coin. One woman between them.
Who will win? The one who looks the part of the scarred man who has a true heart?
What type of woman who ignore the man who flashes cash, has a private plane, limo and driver and has the looks over a man whose appearance is damaged.

Where I got the idea:

wanted to write a story where the pretty male was the villain and the scarred man was the hero
Also wanted enthic cultures to play a role - Indian v gypsy

Trope:
woman in jeopardy

Part of a series?
yes

What is the twist? Why is this story different?
the woman in distress believes in rescuing herself. These guys are just in her way

Overriding theme:
good vs. evil
Look beneath the surface to find truth

How many words are you anticipating?   100,000

How many words was the finished product?   80,000

Are you aiming for a specific NY line? Have you checked their storyline requirements?

Notes:

EXTERNAL ARC

What is the problem or the idea behind the story? Save the girl. Get the bad guy.	Must be quantifiable. The reader must be able to see, touch, feel the goal. The world must be saved, the victim must be rescued, the ark must be recovered.
Why do the H/H need each other? Sexual attraction is present. Hero doesn't want a relationship with any woman, Likes being a lone wolf Heroine is trapped by her heritage. A non-gypsy might be tolerated but a federal government agent would not. Plus he thinks He is in charge	**Are the h/h goals going to clash?** In genre writing, the h/h must have conflict between them. Otherwise what is keeping them apart? To illustrate this: if hero is a firefighter, the heroine must be an arsonist. Or if these two people were on a desert island, devoid of external conflict why aren't they together?

Who? Characters	
Cezi - heroine	26, drop out
John - hero	34, lone wolf
Cain - villain	

What? Goals
Heroine - wants to be CSI, wants to be with her family and away from them at the same time.
Hero - Doesn't want his life to change.
Villain - wants to be rich, hates women

Why? Motivation
heroine - doesn't fit in with family nor with outside world, wants to belong
hero - sister died - can't commit
vilain - girl who got away

Why Not? Conflict
Heroine - no education, can't live on own - trapped by rules
hero - job - family
villain - mother meth whore - dumped by other women in his past

What is the ticking time bomb? A story that can be resolved in 2 years has no urgency. Why must this happen now?   Cezi's life in danger - must stop sex trade

Are there consequences if the story does not get resolved?   YES - Cezi dies

Is your antagonist/villain as strong as your protagonist? A super hero needs a super villain. Every fight must be worthy. Whether it is good vs evil (*Harry Potter*), man against nature (*Titanic*) or man vs the supernatural (*Alien*) the reader must be both engaged and worried.

INTERNAL ARC

Title: <u>Hell On The Heart</u>   **Genre:**   Romantic suspense

At the beginning of the story what is the Hero's internal goal? to keep to himself and never let anyone in	**How does this change?** **What does the hero really want?** to be able to love a woman and protect her
At the beginning of the story what is the **heroine's internal (emotional) goal?** to fit in to the gypsy community without being forced to marry anybody who danced	**How does this change?** **What does the heroine really want?** to be valued - to have someone see she worth
Why does the hero want this? to make up for his sister's death	**Why does the heroine want this?** her life is on hold - she will never be more than she is if she can't make changes
What is keeping the hero from his goals? pain - can't go through caring about someone and losing them again.	**What is keeping the heroine from her goals** fear - censure by the community fear - of leaving beliefs - gypsy without a community is rudderless

Remember conflict must be resolved by the characters, not external coincidence. In order for conflict to be sustained throughout the story, thumb screws must be tightened, road blocks must be constructed and the light at the end of the tunnel, must be an oncoming train.

Weak motivation, weak conflict make a weak story. Motivation must be deeply compelling. The key is to go for fear. What does the character fear to the very bones of his existence? The outer story answers the question what does the hero/heroine want. The inner story answers the question why. Almost all internal motivation is about self-concept and the belief of higher self-worth. Internal conflict is what prevents the character from achieving true self-worth? How does the character feel about himself? Why?

SCENE GRID – CALL TO ADVENTURE

Cezi in tree hiding from bad guy who manhandled Cain circled below trying to seduce her out of her hiding place. When she doesn't appear, two guys with guns and night vision glasses show up to help Cain look. Cezi texts for help.	We find out Cain's motivation and career. Takes girls to Mexico, sells into the sex trade. We also find out some of his character and motivation. They locate Cezi in the tree.	Cezi climbs down out of tree to avoid being shot. Cain recovers his possessions, but is intent on revenge. She is rescued by family, but without the outcome she expects.
John arrives at work in DC to discuss young women's abduction cases. A call comes in from his guy in the FBI about a murder in Armadillo Creek Texas that involves a black limo. He and his partner, D'Sean leave DC to check it out.	John and D'Sean arrive in Armadillo Creek meet with Sheriff's dept who convey. Their dislike of the gypsies and assure the men that a black limo had nothing to do with the murder. John and D'Sean are disgusted. But the Sheriff's office sends them to the Romney's	

FIRST PAGE CHECKLIST

Title: Hell On The Heart

_√__ Does the first sentence/paragraph grab the reader and pull them into the story?

_√__ Does the first sentence/paragraph ask a story question?

_√__ Does the first page immediately evoke emotion? How?

_√__ Is the main character in jeopardy or a victim of undeserved misfortune?

_√__ Is the main character likeable? Funny? Nice?

___ Is the main character good at what he/she does?

_√__ Is the hero heroic? This may not be required for all fiction but for the romance
writer it is.

_√__ Is there a definable external goal? What is it? Save the girl
_√__ Does the reader know the geographic location of the story?

_√__ What time of day is it? What time of year? Have you shown it?

_√__ Does the reader know when the story is set? What century? What year?

_√__ Does the reader know whose POV begins the first scene?

_√__ Does your plot combine familiarity with a twist?

_√__ Have you as the author begun the story in the manner you will continue?
    Or will the reader feel cheated if the story takes an ugly turn?

___ If the first page is part of a prologue, does the prologue reflect
    where the emotional pain began for the hero/heroine?

CALL TO ADVENTURE CHECKLIST

Title: Hell On The Heart

_√_ What is the compelling reason the hero/heroine accept the call? His career/her jeopardy

_√_ Many genres, like Romance, must have page one begin with the action in order to draw the readers into the story immediately. As a result the ordinary world is woven in as backstory in small pieces. Does the reader know what happened the day/week the story opened?

_√_ Is there a ticking time bomb? The Call to Adventure must have an immediate time frame.

_√_ Is the external arc clear for both the hero and the heroine?

_√_ Is the external goal quantifiable? Not esoteric. Not will the hero/heroine find love?

_√_ Is the internal goal clear for both the hero and the heroine?

_____ Does the reader understand what the hero must undergo/change to obtain his goal?

_√_ Is the internal goal/emotional arc clear for the heroine?

_√_ Does the reader understand what the heroine must undergo/change to obtain his goal?

_√_ What is keeping the hero from achieving his external goal?

_√_ What is keeping the heroine from achieving her external goal?

_√_ Do the h/h have conflict between them that cannot be solved by a conversation?

_√_ What is keeping the h/h apart beyond external conflict?

_√_ Does the Call to Adventure answer the question WHO? Characters.

_√_ Does the Call to Adventure answer the question WHAT? Goals.

_√_ Does the Call to Adventure answer the question WHY? Motivation.

_√_ Does the Call to Adventure answer the question HOW? Conflict.

_√_ Has someone refused the Call to Adventure? Who?

_√_ What would happen if the call was refused? If life goes on as before, your story lacks urgency, motivation and conflict.

_____ In romance a cute meet is optional, but the hero/heroine must meet within 50 pages.

_√_ Have you as the author laid out the consequences the h/h do not meet their goals?

THE HERO CHARACTERISTICS

Title *Hell on the Heart.*

Hero

Name: AGENT JOHN STILLWATER	Age: 35	Nickname: Why: *Tonto joke*
Height: 6'	Weight: 185	Tattoos ARM BAND TARANTULA ON BACK
Hair color STRAIGHT BLK	Eye color BLK	
Education: BS	Military service: SEAL	
Occupation: FBPA AGENT	Previous jobs:	
Divorced: No	Widowed: No	
Religion:	Higher Power: INDIAN SPIRITUAL BELIEFS	
Hobbies:	Quirks:	

Core beliefs:	
Lives where: DC	Why: JOB IS THERE

Accent: NO	
Rich: no	Poor: no
How does he feel about money? *Not overly concerned. There is enough.*	
What is his personal motto? *Save those weaker than himself. Protect Defend. country*	
Physical flaws/body image: *- body marked up from gun wounds, bombings, etc - Dedicated NOT VAIN*	

Glasses: no	Favorite body feature:
Parents: dead	Brothers and sisters: Scattered - Dyani - dead
Children: no	Does he want them? *not really*

THE HERO CHARACTERISTICS

Hero

Social status: *Middle class - but outsider - Indian heritage - warrior mentally*	
Feelings about family: *Keeps his distance likes being lone wolf*	
Hair - long or short: *Short*	Style:
Does he resemble an actor? Which actor?	
Makeup: *No*	Jewelry: *No*
What does he fear the most? *Not being able to save someone he loves*	
What sets him apart? *Dedication*	
Has he had a serious relationship? What happened? *No*	
How important is sex? *He likes it but it is* Into kink? *No* *not that important*	
What does he fantasize about?	
Does he have a special strength or skill? *Being able to read the earth, the sky, the sea*	
Team player: *yes*	Lone wolf: *prefers being alone*
Does he see himself as the one in charge? *Yes*	
What is his vulnerability? *Caring about someone*	
What is his fear? *That he won't be there in time*	

THE HERO CHARACTERISTICS

Hero

Day Job: FBPA Agent	
Is he good at it? Yes	
What kind of car? SUV	
Style of dress: Agents Suits/jackets	**Home décor:** Stark
Dreams:	**Fantasy career:**
How do others see him? in charge, warrior tough	

The Heroine Characteristics

Title _Hell on the Heart_

Heroine	Name: Czigany Romany	Age: 26	Nickname:
			Why: E-Z Cezi; Peata
	Height: 5'2"	Weight: 108	Tattoos: none
	Hair color: blk	Eye color: blk	

Education: Tenth Grade	Military service: no
Occupation: almost licensed P.I.	Previous jobs: none
Divorced: no	Widowed: no
Religion:	Higher Power: Gypsy beliefs
Hobbies: Reads Tarot	Quirks:
Core beliefs: ~~Gypsy Gypsy~~ Gypsy Philosophy	
Lives where: Swallowtail Hollow, Armadillo Creek, Tx	Why:
Accent: no	
Rich: no	Poor: no
How does she feel about money? Has enough money - Money goes into central location. Doled out	
What is her personal motto? I gotta get out of this place	
Physical flaws: none - short	
Glasses: no	Favorite body feature: Ivory skin
Scars: no	Body image: doesn't give it much thought
Parents: father alive mother dead	Brothers and sisters: no

The Heroine Characteristics

Heroine		
Children: *No*	Does she want them? *Yes & no - afraid* *She will die young*	
Social status: *outcast - not married - no children*		
Feelings about family: *loves them - trapped by them*		
Hair - long or short: *long curly*	Style: *loose*	
Does she resemble an actor? Which actor?		
Makeup:	Jewelry: *on special occasion* *decks out in dangling earrings* *+ bangles - boats gold*	
What does she fear the most? *Being alone*		
What sets her apart?		
Has she had a serious relationship? What happened? *No*		
How important is sex? *not* Into kink? *No*		
What does she fantasize about? *being free of family - living a different life*		
Does she have a special strength or skill? *tarot cards*		
Team player: *yes*	Lone wolf: *No*	
Does she see herself as the one in charge? *No*		
What is her vulnerability? *wants to be on her own - afraid to be alone*		

The Heroine Characteristics

Heroine	What is her fear?	
	What does she dream about?	
	What kind of car does she drive? *Jeep* ✓	
	Style of dress: *Casual*	Home décor: *Femine, frilly*
	Day job: *PI*	Good at it: *Yes*
	How do others see her? *Misplaced; smart, defiant, loving*	

The Villain, Nemesis, Antagonist Characteristics

Title: Hell on the Heart

Villain

Name: Cain	Age: 35	Nickname: Why:

Height: 6		Weight: 175	Tattoos no

Hair color dark brown	Eye color brown	

Education: High School	Military service: no

Occupation: Abductor of women	Previous jobs: minimum wage

Divorced: Unknown	Widowed: No

Religion: No	Higher Power: $ $

Hobbies: sings - when he is at his most evil he sings	Quirks:

Core beliefs: protect yourself first

Lives where: Mexico	Why? Protection

Accent: no

Rich: getting there	Poor: no

How does he/she feel about money? loves it, loves it loves it

What is his/her personal motto?

PhysicB27:136al flaws: none - had plastic surgeries to correct

Glasses: no	Favorite body feature: face

Scars: ps ~~no~~	Body image: Perfect

Parents: with mother	Brothers and sisters: unknown

The Villain, Nemesis, Antagonist Characteristics

Children: no	Does he/she want them? no
Social status: Criminal, outcast	
Feelings about family: # Hates family	
Hair - long or short: Longer than normal	Style: Expensive
Does he/she resemble an actor? Which actor?	
Makeup: nothing	Jewelry: outstanding
What does he/she fear the most? Being caught	
What sets his/her apart? Looks, Cunning	
Has he/she had a serious relationship? What happened? Yes - she dumped him for lack of $	
How important is sex? Into kink? almost impotent - unless violent	
What does he/she fantasize about? Blood, power, revenge	
Does he/she have a special strength or skill? no	
Team player: no	Lone wolf: yes
Is he/she in charge? yes	
What is his/her vulnerability? Can't rely or trust others	

The Villain, Nemesis, Antagonist Characteristics

What is his/her fear? *Being caught*	
What does he/she dream about? *$ - Power*	
What kind of car does he/she drive? *none*	
Style of dress: *Expensive*	Home décor: *lives in a room he rarely sees*
Day job: *Criminal*	Good at it: *Yes*
How do others see him/her? *Dangerous, obedient, lives behind a Mask*	

About The Author

Nancy Brophy lives in the beautiful Northwest, married to a Chef whose mantra is: life is a science project. As a result she has chickens and turkeys in her backyard, a fabulous vegetable garden which also grows tobacco for an insecticide and a hot meal on the table every night.

For those of you who have longed for this, let me caution you. The old adage is true. Be careful what you wish for, when the gods are truly angry, they grant us our wishes.

And the payment is always high.

Nancy's body pays for this luxury by struggling not to gain ten pounds a year.

There was never a time when she didn't write. As an award-winning author she has been published off and on for forty years in a wide variety of arenas, some fiction, some not. In 2014, she decided to change her strategy and plans to publish a book a month.

She would love to hear from you with comments and changes to Plotting Your Story Arc that might help other writers. Please contact her at **NancyBrophy@gmail.com** or check out her website at **www.Nancybrophy.com**.

Upcoming Books

Look for Nancy's books on Amazon. *Hell On The Heart* (the example used in the workbook) will be published before the end of the year.

The proposed schedule for the first six months of 2015 are from The Wrong Series:

December 2014 – Hell On The Heart

He wasn't stupid. Fortune-tellers worked in similar ways. Set the stage. Watch for tells – widening of the eyes, facial tics, or other involuntary muscle movements. Crystal ball or tarot cards were props. Everybody had tells. A perceptive grifter knew when their words struck gold. Already she was doing it. Her black eyes bored into his as she took the cards.

January 2015 – The Wrong Brother

This was what lying got you – the wrong brother. But if she couldn't have him, neither could Marlene.

February 2015 – The Wrong Hero

"If this is a chess game, then the one thing you should have been able to predict is that the queen always protects the king."

March 2015 – The Wrong Cop

"It pisses me off I'm attracted to you." He glared at her.
"Well, stop it then."
He sneered. "Great advice. How's that working for you?"
"You're like the wad of gum on the sole of my shoe. Only worth as much consideration as it takes to get rid of you."

April 2015 – The Wrong Lover

Her brown eyes and raspy voice stayed with him. Her taste lingered on his lips. After this fiasco was over, he'd find her. All he knew was that her name was Lily, but it wasn't her name he was after.

May 2015 – The Wrong Husband

"This is a vacation. And we are going to have a fabulous time."

June 2015 – The Wrong Seal

"I employ over one hundred guys, but that's not what I want. I want a man. And you might as well know the truth now. I want someone who is in for the long haul. I refuse to let my heart break when you leave."

WRONG NEVER FELT SO RIGHT

www.ingramcontent.com/pod-product-compliance
Lightning Source LLC
LaVergne TN
LVHW061301060426
835509LV00016B/1664